SECONDARY LEARNING CENTERS

An Innovative Approach to Individualized Instruction

Clifford P. Bee
San Diego State University

Goodyear Publishing Company
Santa Monica, California

media center

To my sons, Jim and Steve
May the ideas of this book find their way into your classrooms.

Library of Congress Cataloging in Publications Data

BEE, CLIFFORD.
    Secondary learning centers.

    1. Individualized instruction. I. Title.
LB1031.B43   371.3'94   80-18719
ISBN 0-8302-8203-3

Copyright © 1980 by

Goodyear Publishing Company, Inc.

Santa Monica, California 90401

Y-8203-5

ISBN: 0-8302-8203-3

Current printing (last digit):
10 9 8 7 6 5 4 3 2 1

Printed in the United States of America

Contents

Preface

The shelves of libraries are filled with a multitude of dusty educational tomes, many of which contain conflicting considerations of profound questions that have essentially remained unchanged from classical times to the present. Many of us have been seeking answers that will enhance teaching and learning in our classrooms from these works. Yet, few have been forthcoming.

One of the most vital concerns in education is how to deal with individual differences. The need to approach and treat students as individuals, each with distinct abilities, interests, achievement levels, and learning styles is undeniable and well documented. The problem has always been how to accomplish the seemingly impossible task of providing for these individual differences at the secondary level.

What makes *SECONDARY LEARNING CENTERS: An Innovative Approach to Individualized Instruction* different from other available books on the subject is that it addresses the issue of meeting the individual differences of students by offering a field-tested approach to teaching: the use of learning centers. Utilizing learning centers is not a new solution. In fact, centers have been used in classrooms for at least one hundred years. Most frequently, however, learning centers have been meeting individual student needs in elementary and special education classrooms. Why they have only recently been introduced in junior and senior high school classrooms is unclear. What is clear, however, is that learning centers are being used by more and more secondary teachers and students with overwhelming success. They have been particularly effective in classrooms with students of diverse learning levels and abilities. Teachers affected by legislation such as mainstreaming are finding learning centers invaluable in meeting the requirements for individualized education programs. Those who advocate the concept of mastery learning of basic skills as a way to meet growing public pressure are also finding success with learning centers.

During the last several years I have worked with hundreds of secondary teachers involved in teaching every subject offered in the curriculum. This book utilizes their experiences and brings together all of the information needed to plan, construct, and implement learning centers in secondary classrooms. It begins with an overview of the need to individualize the teaching-learning process and discusses what this really means to the classroom teacher. However, the book is primarily a practical "how-to-do-it" compilation of ideas developed and refined by secondary teachers. Part I presents these ideas along with information about setting up and utilizing centers; Part II contains actual examples of centers in thirteen subject areas. Thus this book combines a little theory with a lot of practicality. It can serve as a guide to planning, developing, constructing, and implementing learning centers in your classroom. If this results, then the true purpose of the book will have been realized.

Clifford P. Bee

Acknowledgments

This book is unique in that several hundred people contributed to its contents. The many teachers with whom I have worked in seminars and workshops have supplied thoughts and ideas that are found within. I wrote this book for them and with them, and will be forever in their debt. Those teachers who contributed a special idea or learning center and who deserve special recognition include:

Pam Allor
Becky Atkinson
Michele Beauchamp
Carol Danner Benichou
William Beyer
Margaret Bina
Alice Carroll
Marsha Christiansen
Jennifer Clark
Marilyn Connolly
Christine Conrad
Dalyla Creaghe

Susan Emerson
Lois Felshaw
Janell Guidry
Carol Hasart
Karen Hendrickson
Barbara Hirschkoff
Jane H. Kennamer
Shirley Kondo
Nancy Lees
Leon Leyson
Evelyn McKinney
Monice McNutt

Eugene Morgan
Larry Parton
Steve Pollack
Janice Rhoades
Stephen Rodecker
Patricia Ryan
Susan Sandstrom
Donald Schaffer
Joseph Skinner
Robin Spicer
Dewayne Stegner
Judith Stell

Helen Straight
Barbara St. John
Debbie Tadman
Howard Taylor
John Tjaarda
Illean Trautwein
Lydia Tucker
Juanita Washington
Don Welch

I also want to commend and thank Laura Thompson, Production Editor, Goodyear Publishing Company Inc., for her professional help in making this book a reality. Her continuous support and assistance were invaluable.

In addition, I extend my gratitude to Dr. C.M. Charles of San Diego State University who first introduced me to learning centers and who inspired me to undertake the writing of this book. Without his ideas, this book would not have been written.

Most important, I thank my best friend, Biz, for her continuous encouragement, assistance, suggestions, and critical appraisal as the book developed. She was a valued critic, sensitive to both the needs of this writer and to those of students and teachers.

PART ONE

Learning Centers: Overview and Process

WHAT IT MEANS TO INDIVIDUALIZE

Definition of Terms and Statement of Need

Although secondary school teachers are discovering learning centers to be one of the most effective means of meeting the individual learning needs of students, it is important that we, as teachers, have a clear understanding of the general topic of individualization before applying the specific solution, learning centers. Chapter one, then, presents a brief overview of what it means to individualize.

Individualized instruction is one of education's most commonly misunderstood terms. Most teachers and parents use the term casually and freely because it is one of the permanent "in" words of education. Yet, most of us walk away from a discussion of the topic without either fully understanding what we have stated or what we have heard. There are so many ideas and concepts about what individualized instruction is that our first task should be to arrive at a definition so that we can understand one another. Basically, individualized instruction is concerned with the varying learning patterns of students who come to school with a wide assortment of needs; the focus is on different instructional programs for different learners. In short, individualized instruction can be defined as a method of instruction designed to meet each student's continuously changing learning needs relative to interests, achievement levels, abilities, learning styles, and stages of learning. *Personalizing* and *individualizing* are used as synonymous terms in this book. Each refers to differentiating instruction according to the individual differences and needs of each student.

The evidence to support the need to personalize education is prodigious. It is not the intent of this book to present the case for individualization again. However, the following fable and analogy, which present this need in a particularly vivid manner, can serve as a reaffirmation of the necessity for individualized instruction:

THE ANIMAL SCHOOL

Once upon a time, the animals decided they must do something heroic to meet the problem of "a new world." So they organized a school.

They adopted an activity curriculum consisting of running, climbing, swimming, and flying. To make it easier to administer the curriculum, all the animals took all the subjects.

The duck was excellent in swimming, in fact better than his instructor; but he made only passing grades in flying and was very poor in running. Since he was slow in running, he had to stay after school and also drop swimming in order to practice running. This was kept up until his web feet were badly worn and he was only average in swimming. But average was acceptable in school, so nobody worried about that except the duck.

The rabbit started at the top of the class in running, but had a nervous breakdown because of so much make-up work in swimming.

The squirrel was excellent in climbing until he developed frustration in the flying class where his teacher made him start from the ground up instead of from the treetop down. He also developed "charlie horses" from overexertion and then got "C" in climbing and "D" in running.

The eagle was a problem child and was disciplined severely. In the climbing class he beat all the others to the top of the tree, but insisted on using his own way to get there.

At the end of the year, an abnormal eel that could swim exceedingly well, and also run, climb, and fly a little had the highest average and was valedictorian.

The prairie dogs stayed out of school and fought the tax levy because the administration would not add digging and burrowing to the curriculum. They apprenticed their child to a badger and later joined the ground-hogs and gophers to start a successful private school.*

"Courtesy of Phi Delta Kappa, Inc."

Imagine the mile run if it began with the firing of a gun and ended at the end of four minutes when another gun went off and everyone had to stop wherever they were. It would be even more startling if about five minutes later another gun went off for the next race and everyone began that race from the same point at which they had ended the previous one.

By repeating such a process, we would guarantee the development of cumulative deficits for some runners as they fell progressively further behind after each successive race. As long as time were held constant and

*G. H. Reavis, "The Animal School," *Technical Training*, vol. 2, no. 4 (May 1948): 7.

no source of external assistance or remediation were provided, such a consequence would be inevitable. We would find such a practice ludicrous in track, yet we run our educational programs precisely in this manner. Our purpose in education is to see to it that a certain minimal level of competence is achieved by each learner. To do so, we should logically set levels of achievement as constants and let time act as a variable.*

The variable in the track analogy is time, although time is only one of the elements that is important in the development of an individualized program. Because of the complexity of such a process it is helpful to present a brief overview of the total concept of individualization before going into detail about how to attain it.

The Individualization Process

The following overview provides a look at the sequential steps involved in the individualization process and includes the types of objectives that teachers hope to achieve in the classroom, some strategies available to meet these objectives, the desired ingredients of all strategies, implementation factors, and classroom organization and management processes. A diagram of the overview is presented below.

Step 1: INDIVIDUALIZED LEARNING OBJECTIVES

The first step in developing any instructional program is to decide what students should accomplish. These accomplishments usually are stated in the form of objectives and fall into two distinct categories: behavioral-based learning and experience-based learning.

Behavioral-based Learning

Measurement of a behavioral-based objective can take place in a variety of ways—that is, one can see it, smell it, hold it, taste it, etc. If educators are to be held accountable for student learning, then it is common sense to design and teach content so that student knowledge can be measured. Content in this realm falls neatly into two classifications: cognitive, and psychomotor. The first classification refers to the faculty of knowing. This intellectual

*Lee S. Shulman, "Psychology and Mathematics Education," in *Mathematics Education*, the Sixty-ninth Yearbook of the National Society for the Study of Education, Part I (Chicago: University of Chicago Press, 1970), p. 49.

STEP 1 Individualized Learning Objectives			
BEHAVIORAL- BASED		EXPERIENCE- BASED	BALANCED APPROACH
Cognitive Tasks	Psychomotor Tasks	Affective Tasks	Confluent Tasks

STEP 2 Teaching-Learning Strategies		
LAP Contracts DPT Commercial Learning Centers	Contracts Learning Centers	Combination of strategies

STEP 3 Suggested Ingredients	STEP 4 Implementation Factors	STEP 5 Classroom Organization and Management
Rationale Objectives Activities Materials Evaluation	Students Class Time Subject Area	Study Locations Direction Giving Scheduling Assessment, Feedback, and Record Keeping

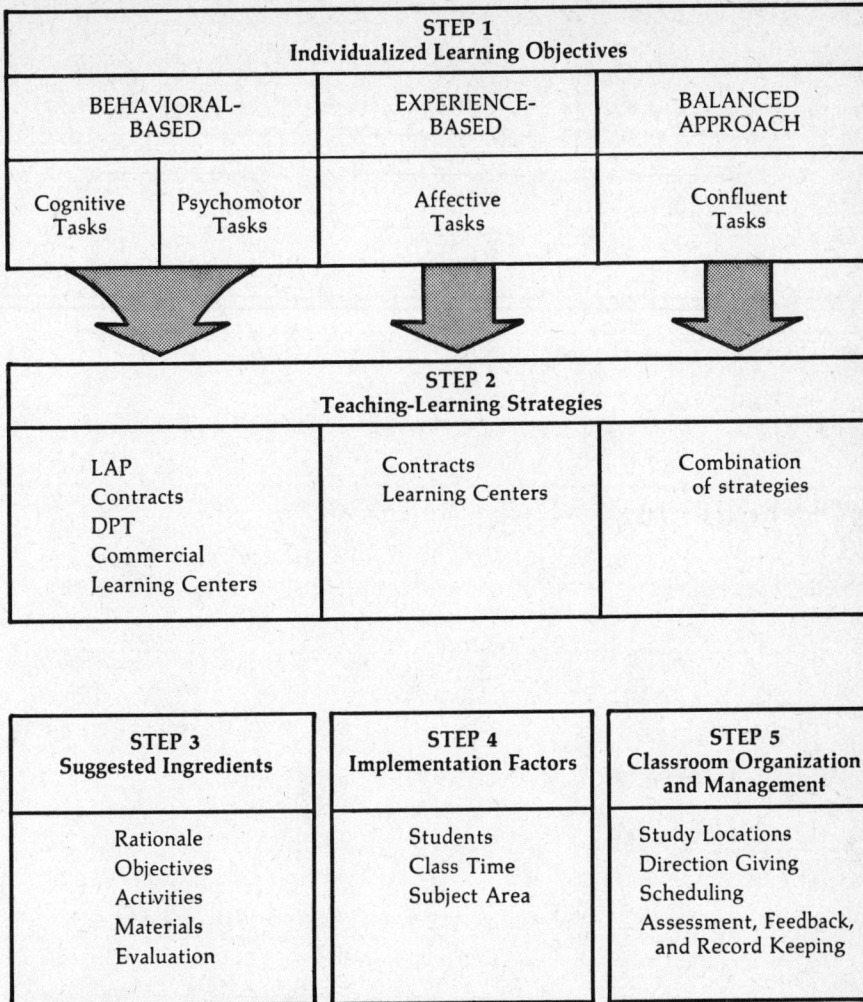

functioning aims mainly at recalling or recognizing specific information in either a verbal or nonverbal manner. Pyschomotor skills, the second classification, are physical movements of the body and, as with cognitive skills, can be either verbal or nonverbal.

Experience-based Learning

Experience-based objectives, although usually intangible, nonetheless are crucial in designing a well-balanced curriculum. These are purposes linked to belief, value, and attitude systems, and are difficult, if not impossible, to measure. Tasks related to this type of learning have been classified as affective in nature.

A Balanced Approach

When making decisions as to what students will learn in school, most teachers will decide on a balanced approach, and seek a way of relating behavioral-based and experience-based learning. The term *confluence* depicts this flowing together or integration of the cognitive, psychomotor, and affective learning tasks.*

An example of confluence might be found in a health and safety class. Suppose that the general goal is that students will understand and be able to perform cardio-pulmonary resuscitation (CPR). Specific cognitive objectives related to patient body placement and proper procedures could easily be designed. This knowledge could be measured in either a verbal or non-verbal manner. The actual physical process of locating proper pressure points and timing could also be stated in terms of objectives and measured as psychomotor skills. The third classification of affective tasks could also become an important contributor to this learning experience. Planned visits to CPR-trained teams at fire departments, police departments, or hospitals would allow students the opportunity to discuss the importance of CPR training with experts. These discussions might be the reinforcement necessary for the students to internalize the positive belief systems or attitudes requisite to achieving the learning task. Obviously this type of experience is important even if it is difficult to measure the degree of achievement.

Step 2: TEACHING-LEARNING STRATEGIES

Once it has been decided what the teaching objectives will be, teachers must decide how to reach them. There are many methods being promoted in the education marketplace today, too numerous to mention here, but the following five approaches seem particularly suited to individualization: learning activity packets, contracting, diagnostic-prescriptive teaching, commercial programs, and learning centers. All five can be used to meet behavioral-based objectives, while contracts and learning centers are especially suited to experience-based learning.

Learning Activity Packets (LAP)

Although there is a multiplicity of terms such as Unipac, teaching-learning units, contract activity packets, modules, and self-paced packages, the general term learning activity packet (LAP) can be used to represent this instructional mode. Although each of the systems named above might be hailed as having unique qualities, the similarities of these strategies far outweigh their differences.

*An overview of confluent education is provided by George Isaac Brown in *Human Teaching for Human Learning: An Introduction to Confluent Education* (New York: The Viking Press, 1971).

A LAP is an instructional unit designed to teach one or more concepts, skills, or ideas and is structured for individual student use. Although the teacher can be an integral part of a LAP, serving in the roles of facilitator, counselor, and evaluator, the unit is usually designed for independent study based upon the individual needs and interests of the student.

The LAP utilizes objective statements in a structured format in terms of "What must be achieved." In terms of "How the achievement will take place," the LAP can provide alternative means. There might be a variety of ways to accomplish an objective and the greater the latitude in providing learning experiences, the greater the prospect of success with each individual student.

Contracting

Contract teaching brings a uniqueness to the instructional process with a major focus on the individual learner. Often integrated with other teaching-learning techniques, it involves close consultation between student and teacher because it takes two parties to make a contract. The contract is a written or oral agreement stating the work to be accomplished by the student, often denoting specific activities, materials, and time parameters. Once the learning contract is agreed upon, the student assumes responsibility for the learning tasks. This strategy curtails the pressure to have all students at the identical achievement level within a curricula area by focusing on individual pacing, readiness, materials, interests, and needs.

Diagnostic-Prescriptive Teaching (DPT)

In essence, diagnostic-prescriptive teaching (DPT) is devoted to finding out "Where the student is" (diagnosis) and designing a plan of instruction to take him or her from that point toward the intended objective (prescription). Usually the teacher has the student take a pretest to discover the level of competence related to a set of established learning objectives. This process allows the student to skip over the study involved in meeting objectives already obtained so that concentration can be given to the specified objectives yet to be achieved.

Commercial Programs

The design of this book is to provide a practical and workable solution to individualizing within the self-contained classroom, thus it is not appropriate to get caught up in the alphabet soup world of large formalized systems of instruction such as IGE (Individually Guided Education), AEL (Adaptable Environments for Learning), IPI (Individually Prescribed

Instruction), SRA (Science Research Associates), and PLAN (Program for Learning in Accordance with Needs). Yet it is important to mention these commercial programs. Many of the systems are complex and costly and a school interested in their adoption and implementation might be required to make a collective decision binding a total staff to a program, rather than allowing the single teacher options. However, developers have invested many dollars and much time in creating viable curricular materials, and any teacher interested in expanding and improving a program to individualize instruction should constantly be on the lookout for adoptable or adaptable concepts and materials.

Learning Centers

The term *learning center* is another of the magical words in education. To some, it means a structural complex housing a library and media center. To others, it is a depository of education wares often located in a central district facility. In this book, however, it is a teaching-learning concept of considerably smaller dimensions, usually located in a self-contained classroom. Its purpose is to introduce, reinforce, and/or expand explicit learning experiences in an individualized learning format. Countless teachers have discovered success in achieving classroom learning objectives with this mode of instruction. As the major focus of this book is on the power of learning centers, they will be discussed in detail in later chapters.

Step 3: SUGGESTED INGREDIENTS

This third step in the process of building an individualized learning program introduces those basic elements usually included in any instructional program. Because this is a composite of suggested ingredients, there is some overlap with both steps one and two. Regardless of the type of instructional program designed and implemented, following these guidelines should prove helpful to both teachers and students.

Rationale

There are few students who enjoy working and studying without knowing the purpose of their efforts. Common courtesy, reinforced by sound principles of psychological learning theory, is reason enough to provide a rationale for each instructional program. A brief statement relating the nature of the program and the reason for studying it should be the first element of any new instructional unit. Although it can be short, this introduction should be written in an easy-to-read manner so that students will be able to comprehend its purpose. Included should be answers to the ever present and perplexing questions of *Why?*, *What?*, and *How?*:

> *Why* are we studying this?
>
> *What* will be included in our study?
>
> *How* does this fit into the overall scheme of the curriculum?

Objectives

Although this element was considered in step one, it is important to mention goals and objectives again as ingredients. Statements of long-range goals and more short-range, performance-based objectives are critical to both teacher and students. Without a declaration of what teachers want students to accomplish, learning activities can turn out to be counterproductive. To attain accountability in a teaching-learning environment requires careful planning. The use of special verbs of action and performance can greatly aid in achieving this element in instructional planning.*

Activities

The activities that students experience during any teaching-learning situation represent the core of the process. If these activities are well planned and related directly to designed objectives, a giant step will have been taken toward accomplishing the stated purposes. Teachers can enhance the learning experience by offering as many alternative activity choices as possible for meeting learning objectives. The feeling of having control over one's own destiny is an important learning principle and this feeling is advanced when choice is available. One way for teachers to approach this important ingredient is to "brainstorm" as many approaches as they can that will be related to or accomplish each objective.

Materials

The importance of materials cannot be stressed enough. As activities are considered the core of the teaching-learning process, materials represent the core of these activities. Although it would be an impossible task to even begin to list a sampling of the materials and media available, they can be divided into two categories: teacher-made materials, and commercially prepared materials. Usually it is more fitting to use teaching-learning materials

*A more complete discussion of the purpose of objectives and how to write them is presented in Chapter four.

that have been prepared by the teacher who also wrote the objectives. Frequently, however, commercial materials can be adapted and in some cases even totally adopted for special classroom use. The use of commercial materials and media in secondary classrooms has increased significantly in the last several years, particularly in the area of individualizing instruction. Educational supply stores are increasing in number and offer the latest in classroom materials. For teachers who do not have access to these educational supermarkets, catalog houses offer a smorgasbord of wares for the classroom. However, it is advisable to go slowly regardless of purchasing power. Field tests with students, using a limited purchase, should be conducted prior to buying in volume. Remember that the worth of any material or media is how it enhances learning aimed at a predesigned objective.

Evaluation

The final ingredient in developing a total instructional program is evaluation. Frequently this stage is avoided because it is misunderstood. Part of the problem rests with the academic rigor that is often associated with evaluation. A notion of threat and a feeling of apprehension is sometimes created when one encounters the professional evaluator's plethora of statistical phenomena. Although educational evaluation can be an imposing and complex process, it can also be dealt with in a more simple manner.

Basically, teachers want to know whether or not students have achieved the designed instructional objectives. The model is a simple, straightforward one:

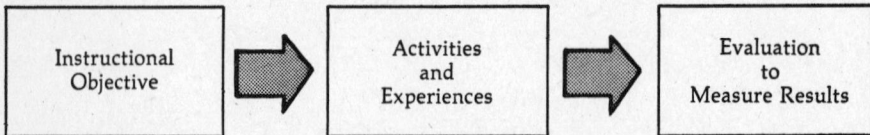

Instructional Objective	⇒	Activities and Experiences	⇒	Evaluation to Measure Results

Its purpose is to assist both teachers and students in making decisions regarding the instructional objectives that need to be accomplished. Because this is a brief overview of the suggested ingredients for an evaluation program, only three basic modes of gathering data are mentioned:

1. *Pretests:* These tests are given in order to determine the status of the student in regard to various skills, aptitudes, or achievements that correlate to instructional objectives. A pretest helps to avoid replication and duplication of learning where it is not warranted. If a student already comprehends the content, the student should be allowed to move on to new ventures.

2. *Self-tests:* A self-test aids students in monitoring their own learning. Usually such tests are optional activities within an instructional program.

The students frequently check their own answers and results are usually not recorded. Help can be requested and provided in light of the results of self-tests.

3. *Posttests:* Some of the misinformation that exists concerning individualized instruction is that posttests cannot be used to measure or gauge student achievement. Nothing could be further from the truth. Any of a number of types of tests can be used in this regard. Examples of tests that might be employed by teachers following the completion of an individualized learning program or set of objectives include oral reports and discussions; teacher-made short answer, essay, or multiple choice tests; study sheets and student workbooks; and standardized tests that have been developed for local school district, state, or national use. Evaluation should be designed to aid decision making and to help achieve the desired objective.

Step 4: IMPLEMENTATION FACTORS

One of the most important decisions in developing an individualized instruction program involves forming a philosophic position toward the approach that has been selected and organizing procedural steps for initiating the process. The factors of students, class time, and subject area are discussed as a basis for formulating a personal philosophy and for selecting procedures that will enhance a program's success. Although a general overview of implementation factors is provided, particular emphasis is given to their importance in the use of learning centers.

Students

Many students work well on their own and will accomplish more within an individualized framework than within a more conventional setting. This has been documented time and again by teachers who have experienced the power of individualized strategies to attract and "turn-on" learners.

In any classroom, however, the teacher's purposes will dictate who will work at individualized programs or centers. A center may be designed for total class use, such as introducing core content that every class member should know. Another center may be designed for selected student use, such as remedial work or enrichment of basic course content. Depending on the type of center developed, its purpose, and the individual needs of the students, there might be several students working at centers while the remainder of the class is in a large group setting. It is important to remember, however, that allowing students to work in any individualized program is a privilege and not a right. In other words, a common sense approach should be used in deciding who will receive the privilege and who will not. A written statement of rules of conduct will go far to advance correct usage.

Class Time

Chapter two of this book presents a general model of how to fit learning centers into the class time available during the semester or school year. On a day-to-day basis, some teachers organize their lesson plans so that time is set aside regularly for individualized work. Other teachers adjust work time at centers according to individual learner needs as they arise. There does not appear to be any consensus among teachers as to the best way to schedule daily class time. It is a personal decision, based on experimentation and experience with classroom centers and other individualized programs. We do learn by experience!

In addition to questions regarding the scheduling of class time for center usage, the issue of the length of time students should have at any one center is often raised. Obviously the answer to this question is contingent upon the objectives and activities created for the center. It is important to realize that time should not be the dictating factor in achieving individualized learning objectives. Time should not, however, be indefinite. Students should be alerted that a learning program is typically completed in a certain amount of time. Again, experience will provide a guide in setting a target completion date. This avoids having a student take several weeks to complete material usually completed in several days. Avoiding time limits, but providing realistic time parameters, can be helpful to both teacher and student.

Subject Area

When centers are used in the classroom, decisions must be made whether the content to be studied will be general or specific. In other words, will an entire unit of work be placed in a center format or just a specific portion? For example, a series of centers could be developed for a unit on library skills. The total content of the unit would be set up for all students. The basic objectives would be the same for each student in the class with the specific activities and time elements serving as the individualization variables. On the other hand, the general topic of library skills could be taught in a large group setting with centers used to focus on selected areas within the larger topic, such as correct usage of the card catalog and library reference materials. Those with limited experience in working with centers might find it helpful to begin with smaller topics on a more specific level and gradually expand to the larger, more general, use.

Step 5: CLASSROOM ORGANIZATION AND MANAGEMENT

Each of the components listed under step five is explained in detail later in this book. Therefore, only a brief description is provided here to serve as an introduction to each. There is also overlapping of these components with the ingredients and factors of steps three and four, but it is often helpful to separate these "housekeeping" matters from those more philosophical aspects of implementing individualized instruction.

Study Locations

The locations for any individualized study, and learning centers in particular, are obviously dependent on a number of variables. For example, the type of instructional program selected, the storage areas needed, the use of electricity for various centers, the size of the classroom, and the availability of additional study areas in the school are several factors that must be considered. Chapter three presents an overview of using a single classroom for many learning centers.

Direction Giving

One important result of utilizing an individualized program for student learning is that teachers receive some "free" time. That is, teachers turn over some instructional time to the individualized strategy selected. In order to reap this "free" time, however, teachers must emphasize direction giving. Directions must be clearly stated so that students can begin and complete a program of activities without interruptions. Help sought from the teacher should relate to learning problems and not faulty directions. Chapter four presents a detailed overview of the direction-giving component.

Scheduling

Any decision related to scheduling students into an individualized learning program is contingent upon the type of program being used and the number of students involved. Chapter six provides an overview of scheduling practices along with several specific examples employed by secondary teachers.

Assessment, Feedback, and Record Keeping

Constant assessment and feedback to students working in an individualized format is critical. The specific amount of assessment and feedback is related to the type of instructional program, the complexity of objectives, and the individual student's needs. Both written assessment and feedback in the form of tests and oral student-teacher discussions can be utilized. The keeping of records indicating progress is also important to an individualized learning program. Both student and teacher can assume a role in keeping accurate records. Besides discussing scheduling, Chapter six covers the topics of assessment, feedback, and record keeping.

Summary. This chapter has done the following:

1. Defined the concept of individualized instruction
2. Reaffirmed a rationale and support for its use in the secondary school
3. Introduced and described the following sequential steps that must be considered in the individualization process:
    a. Individualized learning objectives
    b. Teaching-learning strategies
    c. Suggested ingredients
    d. Implementation factors
    e. Classroom organization and management

2

LEARNING CENTERS AS AN INSTRUCTIONAL APPROACH

For years teachers in secondary schools, both junior and senior highs, have been told, and have concurred, that instructional programs to meet the individual needs of students are requisite. Recently, a distinguished California commission took several years to investigate the major problems facing intermediate and secondary schools throughout the state.* A major recommendation of this study was the need for personalized education programs based on the premise of individual diversity and self-development. Although this recommendation was important and commanded national attention, an investigation of most local school district or state curriculum guides, no matter what the printed date, would indicate a similar goal and philosophy. The pronouncement, although influential, was not new or innovative. The concern of teachers now is not to rediscover the need to personalize teaching and learning in the secondary schools, but to identify solutions that work. Learning centers, as part of a balanced program, are one of the solutions that have been successful and have gained favorable responses from both teachers and students.

*Rise Commission, *The Rise Report* (Sacramento, California: California State Department of Education, 1975).

Implementing Change

Some innovations are thought to be a panacea for any or all educational problems. However, this bandwagon approach of total adoption without weighing consequences, more frequently than not, produces discontinuance or abandonment of an idea. This is too bad since many innovations, if approached correctly, can prove worthy. Before an educator becomes excited about any possible solution, attention should be given to practical considerations such as:

> Is the method to be adopted better than the one currently in use?
>
> Can the method be put into use efficiently?
>
> How effective will it be?
>
> Will the idea necessitate in-service and preparation time? How much?

These, along with other considerations and consequences, are critical and should not be overlooked when change is in the offing. The use of the adoption/change flowchart that follows might save a teacher much wasted time and effort. Each stage in the process serves a gatekeeper role so that a new concept or idea receives serious consideration and approval prior to adoption.

Slogans such as "Change for the Sake of Change" and "Innovation at all Costs" should not be the rallying cries for adopting possible solutions. However, change for the improvement of the teaching-learning process should be a constant goal of the entire educational establishment.

Definition and Overview

One change that has been proven successful is the implementation of learning centers. Although often used to describe a building housing various educational supplies, the term *learning center* is used throughout this book to refer to an instructional approach designed to introduce, reinforce, and/or expand explicit learning experiences. The centers themselves are locations in a classroom or other appropriate space where students can go to take part in a specific learning activity. These activities are based on individual learner needs or interests related to basic goals and objectives, specific skills and concepts, and exploratory and enrichment experiences.

Instructional student centers, another name for learning centers, have been used since the late 1800s when special learning materials were provided for the blind by the Library of Congress. Today's elementary students

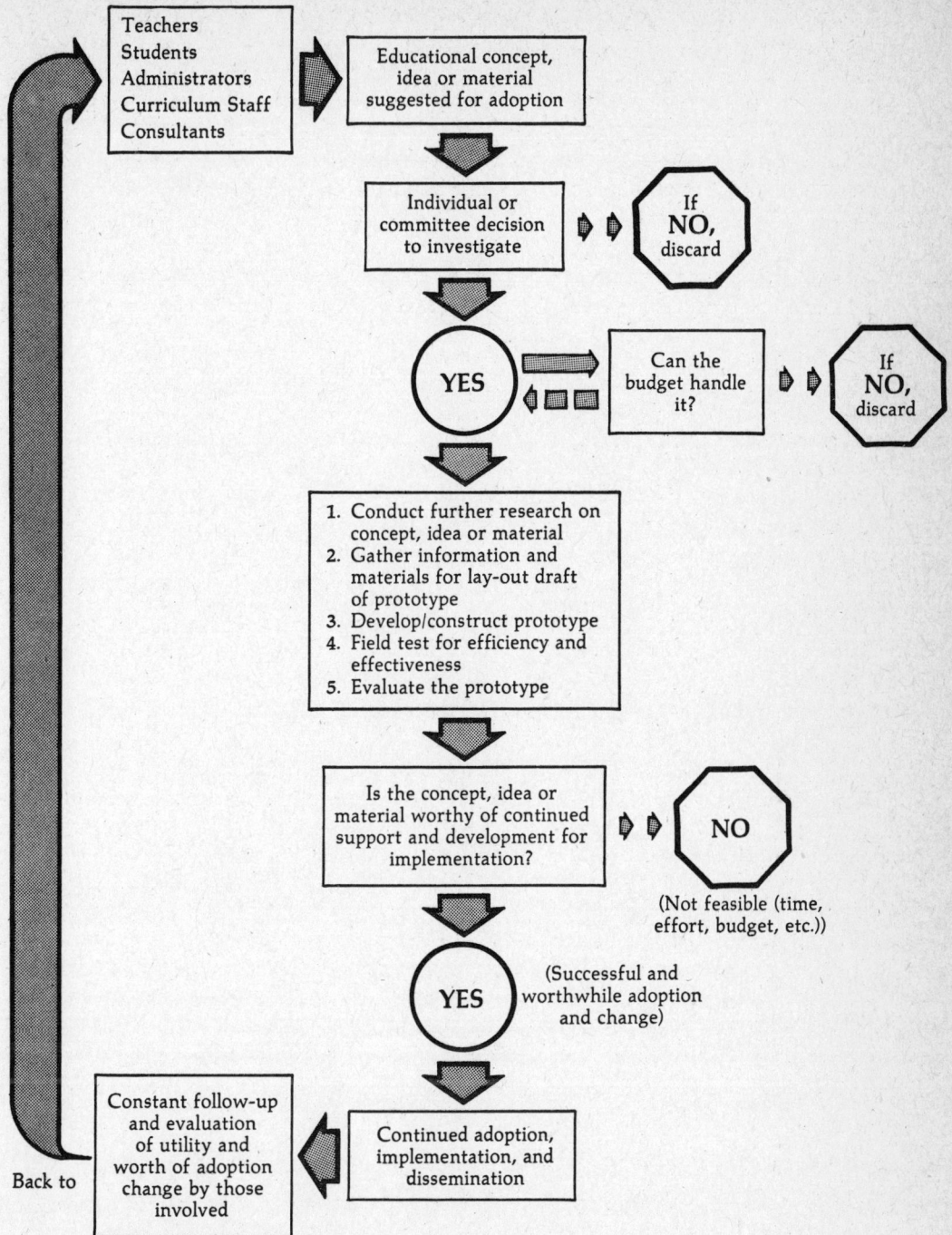

Teachers
Students
Administrators
Curriculum Staff
Consultants

Educational concept,
idea or material
suggested for adoption

Individual or
committee decision
to investigate

If
NO,
discard

YES

Can the
budget handle
it?

If
NO,
discard

1. Conduct further research on
   concept, idea or material
2. Gather information and
   materials for lay-out draft
   of prototype
3. Develop/construct prototype
4. Field test for efficiency and
   effectiveness
5. Evaluate the prototype

Is the concept, idea or
material worthy of continued
support and development for
implementation?

NO

(Not feasible (time,
effort, budget, etc.))

YES

(Successful and
worthwhile adoption
and change)

Constant follow-up
and evaluation
of utility and
worth of adoption
change by those
involved

Continued adoption,
implementation, and
dissemination

Back to

are being reared on the learning center concept through special interest centers, science corners, listening/reading posts, book corners, and learning stations. These approaches, in addition to being time tested, meet the criteria of validity and reliability. They do what they were designed to do, and do it well.

It is the use of learning centers at the secondary level that is new. Many secondary teachers who have attended in-service workshops or graduate curriculum classes have had interesting reactions when hearing about the learning center concept. Comments have included:

> I remember learning at centers when I was in elementary school. It's a self-motivating device.

> I know elementary teachers who are currently using the center idea. Students love it.

> It's certainly not a new idea.

> Centers in the secondary classroom? I never thought of that!

The most important comment, however, came from those teachers who had used centers: "They work."

Dividing Instructional Time

Secondary teachers who have used learning centers to individualize instruction in their classrooms have often organized the teaching-learning process by using three natural breakdowns. This format is known as the 1/3, 1/3, 1/3 approach. It involves the total time a student spends in a class, throughout a semester or school year, and divides the instructional time into three general modes: teacher-directed instruction, teacher-student interactive instruction/learning, and student-directed learning. Perhaps only one or two of the approaches will be used during a particular day or week. Yet at the end of a school semester, equal time will have been devoted to all three teaching-learning approaches. Balance is the key.

TEACHER-DIRECTED INSTRUCTION

Any class taught by a qualified, professional teacher should offer content presented by that teacher. Contrary to those who might be riding the wave of "Do your own thing," a teacher has the responsibility to become a dispenser of knowledge. Each subject area has particular and basic information that should be presented, in some form, to students and 1/3 of the total time spent in school is not too much time for this type of instruction.

Educators have long been involved in a philosophical debate of content versus method, but this is not the issue here. In terms of this discussion, *content* refers to subject matter that is presented to students in any course. The approach or technique used by a teacher to relate content is referred to as *method*. During the first third segment of class instruction, a teacher might present an idea or meaning (content) by using a lecture or recitation (method). Obviously, the more effectively a teacher can complement content and method, the more effective the teaching and learning.

TEACHER-STUDENT INTERACTIVE INSTRUCTION/LEARNING

The second third of the time devoted to a subject should be dedicated to processing content. This pursuit has been frequently labeled *active learning*. Active learning requires the individual participation of each student in the class and it becomes the responsibility of the teacher during this mode to make certain of this involvement. The premise of this approach is that what a student learns is influenced not only by the relationship established with the teacher, but the relationships established with peers. Group investigations, role-playing, teacher-led discussions, questioning strategies, and small-group activities typify methods of instruction that can be used in this mode, which is also known as the process approach.

Many teachers who use the process approach find it more demanding than their role as dispenser of information. Being a facilitator should not be equated with the concept of nondirected instruction. Quite the contrary, the interaction of students and teachers should be directly focused on the goals or objectives of the class—on the subject matter being studied. This is a time to solidify content, whether the source be teacher or textbook, by using any of a variety of process techniques or strategies, including the following:

analyzing	explaining	organizing	solving
applying	formulating	outlining	summarizing
clarifying	generalizing	paraphrasing	supporting
classifying	illustrating	producing	translating
describing	interpreting	questioning	utilizing
discussing	locating	relating	validating
expanding	making	revising	verifying

STUDENT-DIRECTED LEARNING

The final third of time spent in school is devoted to personalized or individualized student learning. Most local, regional, and state curriculum guides contain a statement that reflects a dedication to developing and implementing a personalized education program for each student in words such as the following:

> We believe that each student should be provided an instructional program which best develops a loyal, effective, self-reliant, active, and happy individual. Further, we believe that each student should have some control over his or her own destiny in pursuing the goals and objectives. . .

Simply speaking, school districts believe that instructional programs should be individualized to some degree. It would be rare to find a teacher, or parent for that matter, who would not agree with this goal. The concern, however, is that there exist few practices for achieving a personalized learning program that can be adopted and implemented with relative ease by the individual classroom teacher. Learning centers are one solution that has been successful as the final third in the 1/3, 1/3, 1/3 approach.

During the last several years, I have worked with hundreds of secondary teachers who have designed, constructed, and implemented learning centers in their classrooms. No subject area in the curriculum has been neglected. Centers have been used for students who are rapid and slow learners, for those who are gifted and those with learning disabilities. They have functioned well in the open classroom and in the self-contained classroom, in a nonstructured and structured environment. In short, many teachers have succeeded in achieving the 1/3, 1/3, 1/3 balance of each component.

Student Response

Two concerns of teachers in relation to learning centers are student achievement and student attitude. Each is a separate issue, but they overlap and influence each other enough to address both together. Although there is no data at this time that supports the thesis that improved school achievement will take place by using learning centers, the reverse is also true. No data exists that reveals that learning centers hinder learning. On the issue of attitude, however, there is some evidence. The attitude of students toward schooling and learning appears to be improved by using the center approach. Many teachers see a direct correlation between attitude and school achievement. They believe if a student's attitude improves, that achievement will also improve. This is difficult to argue.

Some teachers have also sought to enhance student attitude by including them in the planning and construction of learning centers. By delegating some responsibility and soliciting student help in originating ideas and materials, the teacher often gains a classroom partner.

When feedback has been gathered from students, the responses have been overwhelmingly positive. In one case, the question asked of an eleventh grade English class was: "Did you like or dislike this kind of instruction? (Circle one). Tell why." Ninety percent of students responding circled "like." The most prevalent reason for circling "dislike" was that scheduling placed these students at the learning center last. The proposed solution to this problem was "make and use more centers!" Thus, most of the negative responses were really positive ones. Reasons for liking the centers included:

> It was interesting and fun to do.

> It gave me a chance to do things at my own pace.

> I liked it because it gives the individual a chance to have some leeway. He doesn't have to do one particular topic or form of writing.

> I thought it was a good chance to use your creativity.

> It was a more independent study and very instructive. The assignments were short and brief, but direct.

> I like it because I can work at my own speed.

> I liked this type of work because it gave us all a chance to express ourselves in all types of ways. I thoroughly enjoy writing creative papers, and hope to do more in English.

> I like it because it lets the students work at their own speed and it also makes them feel more independent. I have always liked working on my own and I enjoyed the topic in it.

> I like it because you can work at your own speed and independently.

> It allows me to be me. In other words, it doesn't cramp my style!

In another survey, seventh and eighth grade students in a Spanish class reported as follows:

> You can work at your own pace, and the teacher doesn't have to go over the material eighteen million times. It is also more fun than reading out of the Spanish book because we normally don't do anything like that.

> I like learning centers because you get out of study hall.

> I like it because you can do it all by yourself, and you can work the machines and stuff.

> It is easier to work because there aren't that many people around you.

> Because everything's all there.

> I think it is much more interesting this way. You learn faster than if the teacher was teaching you the same information.

I like individual things like that and I think it would be neat to do again.

It was not as boring as regular work and you don't have to repeat things over and over after you've already learned.

Because you learn things you wouldn't normally learn from textbooks. It's interesting. You see pictures and it's fun.

Summary. This chapter has done the following:

1. Discussed practical considerations and presented a flowchart for adopting educational change
2. Introduced the general concept of learning centers as a means of personalizing the teaching-learning process
3. Described the 1/3, 1/3, 1/3 approach to dividing instructional time
4. Presented some student responses to the use of learning centers

WAYS TO USE LEARNING CENTERS

A major objective of the learning center approach to instruction is to personalize learning. Some students will not need to study at all the centers that are set up in a classroom, and other students will need to complete only some of the learning activities at a particular center. Besides flexibility in who will use the centers, this approach provides an opportunity for the introduction of a wide variety of topics. The size, shape, and location of the centers are also variables that can be altered to meet the needs of a specific classroom situation.

Four Types of Centers

The various ways that centers can be used seems infinite. However, all centers can be categorized into one of four basic types: single-subject centers, enrichment centers, remedial centers, and independent-study centers.

SINGLE-SUBJECT CENTERS

The single-subject center is designed to present the content of a specific subject area. This type of center can stand by itself, as a self-contained unit of content, or it can be linked to a common core of content and presented as a supplementary learning tool.

For example, one segment of the curriculum in an English classroom is usually devoted to the writing of a research paper. The entire unit on writing a research paper might be presented by using the center approach. On the other hand, a common core of the topic might be presented by using other teaching-learning approaches with the center method presenting only a portion of the content. Centers used in this manner would offer a personalized learning format to those students who might need work with a particular area of study. Various centers that might be utilized in the investigation and writing of research reports could focus on using the library (e.g., card catalog, reference materials); research paper format (e.g., table of contents, tables, footnotes, bibliography); typing aids (e.g., margins, centering, spacing); and mechanics of writing (e.g., person, tense, abbreviations, punctuation).

Each of these centers contains a specific bit of content that is necessary for each student to know but does not necessarily have to be taught to each student. Since one of the major objectives of the center approach is to individualize portions of the teaching-learning process, centers should be created for the specific learning needs of students in a particular class.

There are several ways in which teachers can decide which students should use specific centers and to what degree. A teacher should recommend a particular learning center, or a set of activities within a center, based on the needs of the individual learner. The personal knowledge a teacher has about a student can be augmented by some type of pretesting instrument, which can help gauge the student's need in an area. Some students might be identified as having the need to study all of the learning activities at a particular center while others might only need to study specific areas.

ENRICHMENT CENTERS

Like the single-subject center, the enrichment center is designed to enhance a student's learning in a particular subject area. Oftentimes a student becomes excited about a subject area covered in class and wishes to explore the content in greater detail, but the teacher, pressed for time by an ever spiraling curriculum and increasing class size, cannot offer the challenge of an enrichment curriculum. The enrichment center provides for this need.

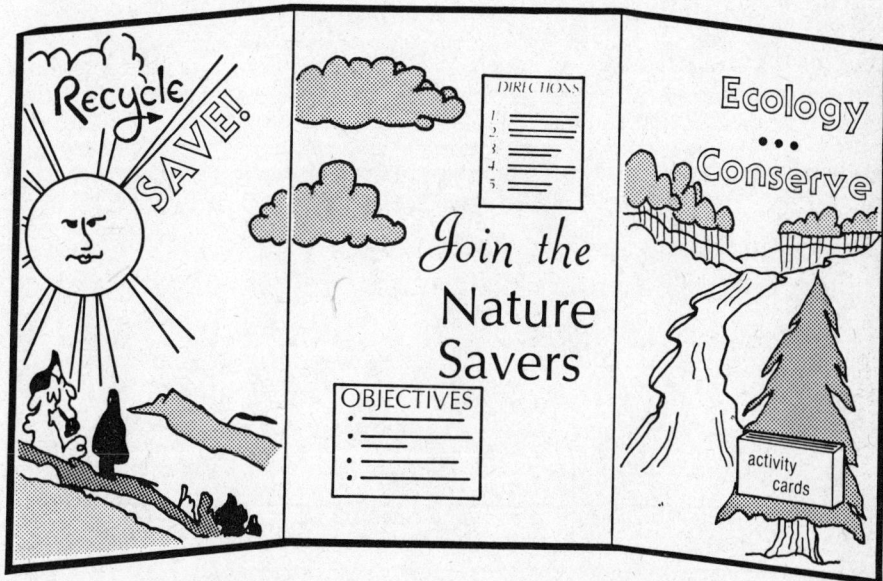

An example of an enrichment center would be one about ecology used in a basic biology class. During class recitation, students are exposed to the topic of ecology, but the rigors of studying the basic principles that influence the existence, behavior, needs, development, and distribution of life do not allow students or teacher time to investigate ecology to the degree that might be desired by a group of students or even one student. A center that provides a variety of alternative learning experiences in this field could produce any number of budding ecologists. This type of center has proven to be successful with many teachers and students, particularly if interest is kindled in a specific area.

REMEDIAL CENTERS

The purpose of a remedial center is to provide special instruction to students who are experiencing some type of learning disability not due to inferior general ability. Learning centers should never be used as a form of punishment.

In many subject areas, content is presented in sequence, as building blocks, with student comprehension and utility contingent upon the mastery of each previous lesson. Sometimes a student can compete successfully in a classroom even though a certain learning unit or lesson was not totally understood. This is rarely the case, however, when content is sequential over the course of a school semester or school year. While most students grasp the content of each curriculum unit and are ready for the next sequence, there are usually some who do not and these youngsters are doomed to fall further and further behind unless the learning deficiency is corrected. One solution to meeting these individual deficiencies has been with the use of remedial learning centers. Basically, the concept of remedial centers is taking the age-old educational phrase "Take the student from where he or she is" and putting this doctrine into practice.

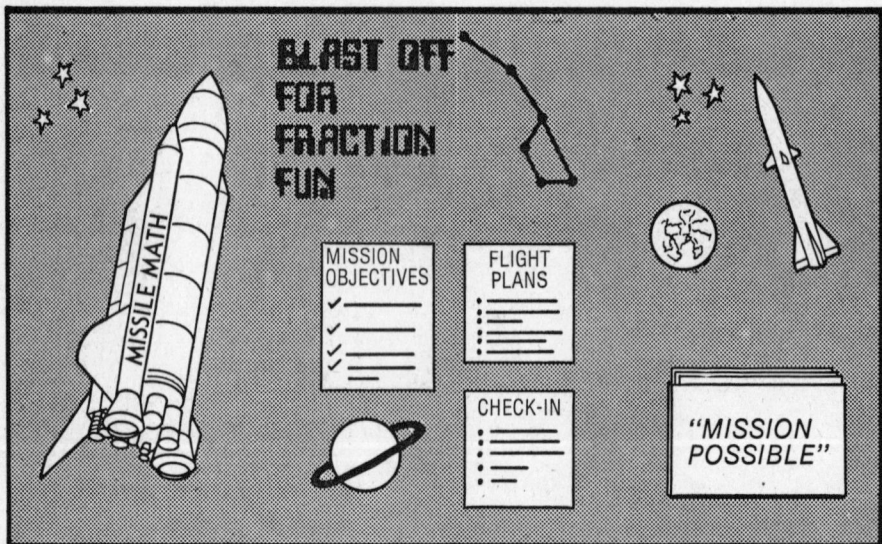

This type of center is particularly suited to mathematics classes. The range of content can vary from the study of basic addition and subtraction to the study of logarithmic and exponential functions. In each case it is necessary to comprehend certain information prior to moving on to new content.

INDEPENDENT-STUDY CENTERS

The independent-study center differs from single-subject, enrichment, and remedial centers in that the content presented may not deal with the basic subject covered in a class. The latitude for treating a subject is much greater with this type of center. Also, as with the enrichment and remedial centers, the content is particularly suited for certain students within each class.

The use of independent-study centers presents wide parameters for individualizing study. If, for example, a student in social studies became interested in a special area of study not normally taught or presented in the basic curriculum of a course, the door would be open for individual investigation and pursuit. Social studies presents many overlapping concepts and skills which are studied in the fields of anthropology, economics, geography, history, political science, and sociology. Few students are provided the opportunity to study in all of these disciplines. As it is, it is usually impossible for a teacher to cover all aspects of a single discipline to the degree desired. Independent-study centers are designed as supplementary approaches for this type of learning.

A specific example of an independent-study center might be one designed to investigate how specific cultural regions of the world are interrelated and interdependent. This center could supplement material introduced in a class or it might stand on its own merits of introducing a separate unit of study. In either case, both students and teacher can link efforts in developing this type of center.

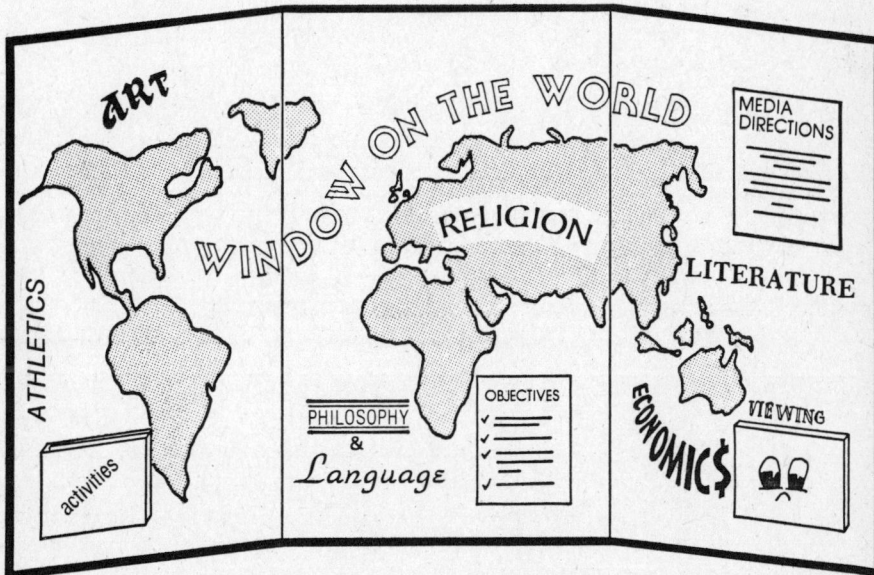

The use of this type of independent study within a classroom has had proven results. It has served as a motivator in kindling or rekindling student interest in a subject resulting in greater student achievement of the core content and objectives of a subject.

The Size and Shape of Learning Centers

Besides being adaptable to many types of activities, and perhaps because of that adaptability, learning centers come in a variety of sizes and shapes. There is no one mold appropriate for all of them. There are, however, several common questions which teachers should ask prior to beginning construction. The answers to these questions should play a large role in determining both size and shape. The questions:

> What are the goals and objectives of the learning center?
>
> Is the center to be used by all students in a class or only those with special needs?
>
> How much content will be contained in the center?
>
> How large is the classroom or location where the center will be stationed?
>
> Will the center be portable or semipermanent?
>
> How much storage space is available?

LEARNING CENTER SIZES

Although actual dimensions will vary a great deal, there are basically two sizes of centers. The first is referred to as a *maxi-center*, the other, a *mini-center*. The choice of size will depend largely on the purpose of the center.

Maxi-Center

The maxi-center is the larger of the two models and is normally designed as a semipermanent device. That is, the center offers a variety of resources, materials, and media equipment, and, because of this apparatus, it generally remains constant to a particular location of the classroom or school. Also, a variety of learning activities are usually provided, covering several goals and objectives, and the maxi-center is typically designed so that several students can be active at any one time.

Mini-Center

The mini-center is a smaller center and is quite portable. Because of its size, it is designed to meet a limited number of objectives and contains little, if any, media equipment. Students can check out the mini-center from a central depository in the classroom or school and work independently on the content. Although a mini-center is usually used for single-student study, this type of center has been used successfully with several students when equipped with games, flashcards, and other appropriate activities.

LEARNING CENTER SHAPES

The shape of a learning center is limited only by its creator's ingenuity and imagination. The following five examples illustrate three typical shapes and two which are not so common.

The Fold-a-Way Center

Many teachers prefer the fold-a-way shape for centers because they are easy to construct, provide ample surface room for illustrations and directions, and are easy to store. This type of center has two or three panels

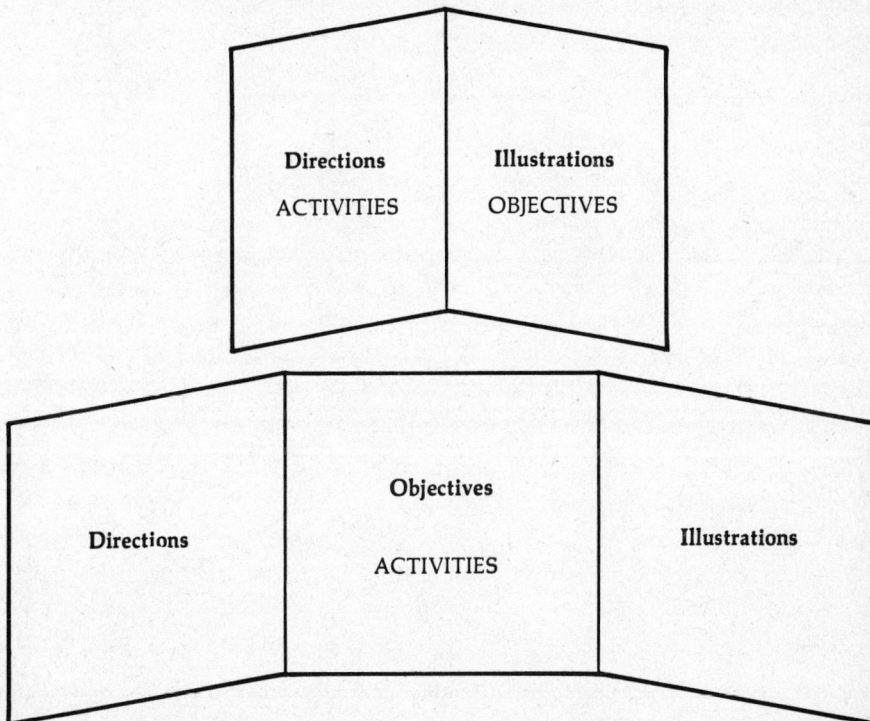

Directions

ACTIVITIES

Illustrations

OBJECTIVES

Objectives

ACTIVITIES

Directions

Illustrations

which are large enough to contain the pertinent information regarding objectives, directions, activity cards, and illustrations.* Additional supplies such as media equipment, software, models, and materials can be stored in containers such as large envelopes or boxes. From one to three students normally can work at this type of center at any one time.

The Four-Sided Center

This type of center resembles four individual study carrels and is often used as such. A simple cut halfway through each of two equal panels such as cardboard, plywood, cork, or pegboard is all one needs to make a four-sided center. The cuts slide together forming four sides. (The same method can be utilized for six- or eight-sided centers if one of the panels is larger.) Permanent panels are not necessary, thus allowing for convenience of storage and assemblage.

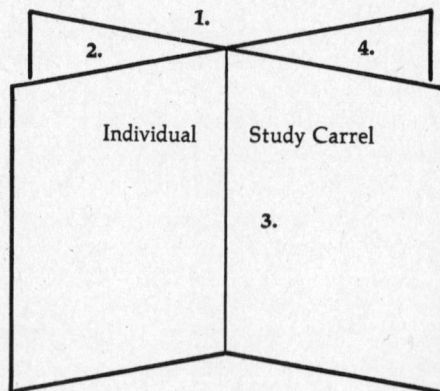

The four-sided center offers the opportunity of developing a sequential learning unit by utilizing each of the four areas (carrels) as steps in a continuing process. Some teachers like to design and develop four different and separate centers while others have found it profitable to have two or more identical centers to meet the needs of students. Normally one or two students can work at each of the four carrels with this design.

The Bulletin-Board Center

Many classrooms do not have the necessary room or furniture to properly use the first two types of centers. In these cases, teachers have discovered a new use for bulletin boards. The basic components of centers (objectives,

*These components of learning centers are described in Chapter four.

directions, and activities) can be included as part of a bulletin-board display on the wall of a classroom. As a bulletin board, it remains a wall display demanding no additional classroom space or furniture until it needs to be used as a center. At that time student desks and/or a small table to hold materials can be pushed to the wall under the display. Obviously the number of students who can use this type of center will depend on both the size of the bulletin board and the size of the classroom. A workable number, however, has been from one to four students.

Unique, Special-Purpose Centers

As stated earlier, centers come in a variety of sizes and shapes; only the imagination limits what can be designed and developed. The following two examples of successful centers illustrate how teachers have constructed unique centers to meet their special needs.

An Industrial Arts teacher in a school with a transient student body found that too much time was being given to repeated teaching of the rules of shop safety. Successful completion of this requirement was needed, however, prior to students working in the shop. The solution to the problem was the design and development of a personalized learning center.

A small box, approximately one foot square, was utilized as a center. Attached to the inside of one side of the box was a small slide projector which swung down ready for use at the pull of a handle. When a set of slides was inserted and projected into the box, several mirrors reflected the picture to a second side of the box which served as a screen.

The uniqueness of the center went further than the box itself, however. The teacher personally took slides of the shop where the students would be working and the equipment that they would actually use. At the bottom of each slide were questions and comments concerning a particular safety rule. Augmenting the pictorial presentation was a cassette tape, which provided directions on how to use the center and additional information for the student on shop safety. A student could sit in one corner of the shop and see the actual equipment described on the tape and pictured on the slides. After a student had used the center, a quick verbal test by the teacher was all that was needed to indicate whether the student was ready to take the shop-safety examination.

This innovative learning center allowed the teacher to spend the majority of the teaching time in the shop and was so successful that a second unit of instruction dealing with reading a micrometer was also developed using the same slide/tape approach.

A center that was more complex to construct but very appealing to students was developed by a high school algebra teacher. He devised an electronic game patterned after television game shows. It was designed as an activity for a small group, although it could be adapted for use by the entire class. The center objectives dealt with linear equations, areas, volumes, factoring, mathematical symbols, and mathematical terminology. The operation of the game was conducted as a quiz show with a master of ceremonies asking various algebraic questions of the contestants or teams of contestants. Each contestant held a simple on/off switch that was numbered and attached to the game board. There were no disputes as to who had the answer first for a question. The order in which the students pressed the switches was indicated on the board via light panels: the first with the answer lit up one light, the second, two lights, et cetera. Answer cards were prepared by the teacher so that a student could serve as the host of this game show. Both the correctness of the answers and the tabulation of scores were controlled by the student host.

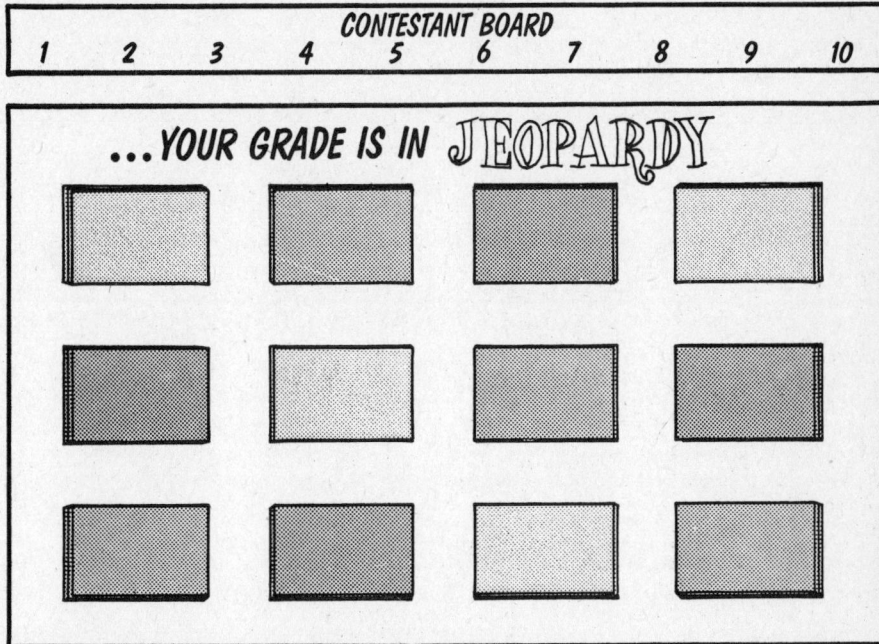

The content of this game could be varied so that it is appropriate for any subject area. It can be used as a single-subject center, an enrichment center, or a remedial center.

The Location of Centers

Where in the classroom should a learning center or centers be located? Answers to this question will vary and there is no one correct answer. The person who is working with the concept for the first time should ask several additional questions before making a final decision:

Will the center interfere with other classroom learning and instruction?

Is electricity needed to run any of the media equipment?

How many students will use the center at one time?

Are supplementary materials needed at the center convenient to the location?

How much storage area is needed?

The answers to these concerns should help one decide on the location for a center.

Frequently a teacher who is just beginning to use the learning center approach will begin with just one center. The center might be situated in a corner of the classroom as in the first illustration below.*

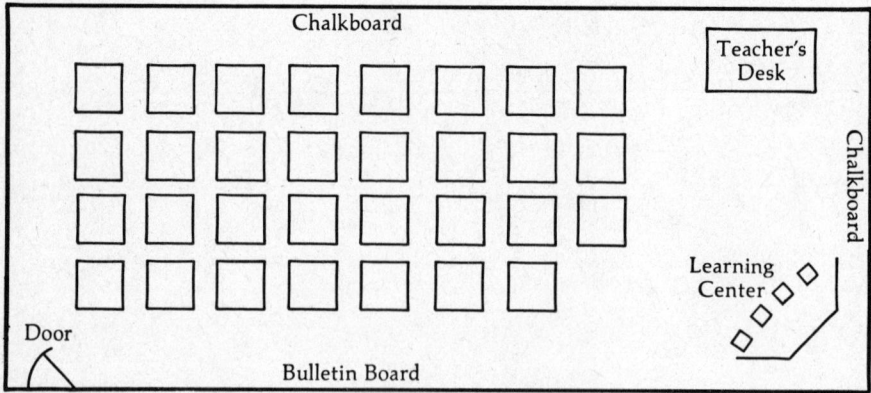

One Center Concept

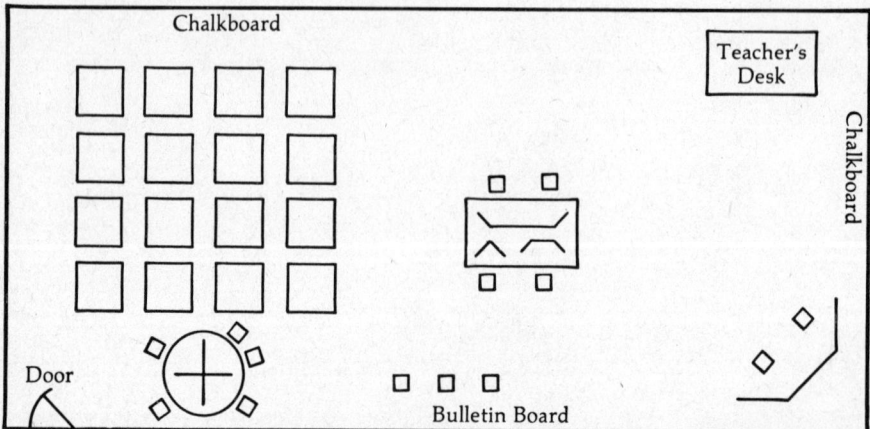

Several Centers Concept

*Although the illustrations depict the center(s) in a classroom environment, they also can be located with success in study halls, instructional media centers, libraries, and any location of a school designed for student use and study.

As teachers become accustomed to using centers, additional centers usually are designed and constructed. When more than one center is set up, the classroom takes on the half and half appearance seen in the illustration at the bottom of page 34.

Many teachers have experienced such great success with learning centers that they have opted to set up their entire classroom as centers (see the Total Centers Concept illustration). Although this approach has been successful for many, teachers beginning to use centers should use caution. Management and record keeping, discussed in Chapter six, are mastered only through experience. Even with the entire self-contained classroom arranged into learning centers, the 1/3, 1/3, 1/3 approach can work well. Teacher-directed instruction and student-teacher interactive instruction/ learning can continue as previously with only the arrangement of students in the room changed. Students can receive teacher-dispensed information and interact with one another from the learning center locations rather than from rows of desks.

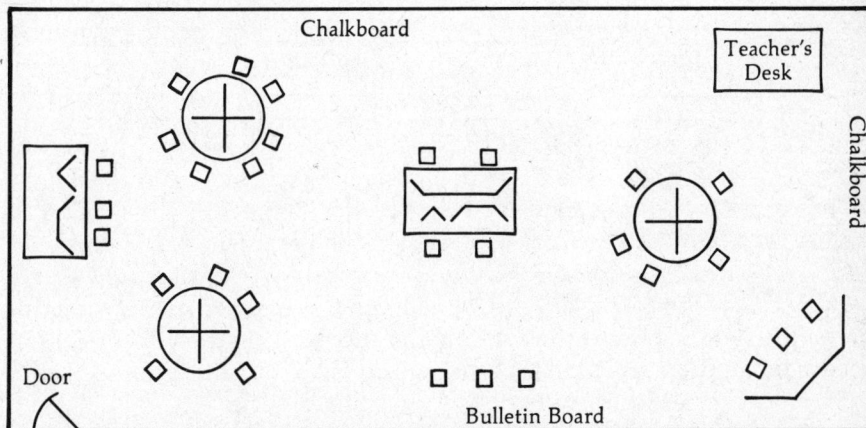

Total Centers Concept

Summary. This chapter has done the following:

1. Introduced the four basic types of learning centers: single-subject, enrichment, remedial, and independent-study
2. Described the two basic sizes of learning centers: maxi-center and mini-center
3. Illustrated the three common shapes of learning centers: fold-a-way, four-sided, and bulletin board
4. Given examples of unique, special-purpose centers
5. Discussed and illustrated ways to locate learning centers within a classroom or school setting

4

COMPONENTS OF
A LEARNING CENTER

It should be stressed once again that the purpose of learning centers is to personalize or individualize the school learning program for students. Of major importance, and included as part of this process, is the freeing of teacher time. As students work at centers in the classroom, teachers should realize time to work with other students who have special needs. Teachers should not have to spend time at the centers defining, explaining, describing, etc. That is the job of the centers, and success is achieved by designing and implementing functional components. The four basic components are: objectives, directions, activity cards, and aesthetics.

Objectives

All too frequently students are confronted with questions such as:

> What are we studying this week?
>
> What will be on the test?
>
> How long will we spend on this topic?
>
> Why should we know this?

They often feel that they need to "psych out" the instructor to discover the intent of a course and for what they will be held accountable. The presentation of clearly stated objectives at the learning center will eliminate many of these student-teacher "psyching" games. By specifically stating what will be studied, these objectives can reduce student anxiety and tension, and interest and learning can be enhanced. Students are more willing to begin a task and work diligently at it if they understand its purpose and can see both a beginning point and an end.

An objective is simply a statement indicating what a student will be able to do after completing a unit of work. It is a statement of intent which is precisely worded, usually using performance or action verbs, and is measurable by some means. If the objectives of a center are affective or experience-based, they usually will be broad-based, long-range, intangible statements which are difficult to appraise or measure with any definiteness. Yet, they are extremely important objectives for the classroom and should not be forsaken simply because they are difficult to measure. Most of the objectives in the single-subject, enrichment, and remedial centers, however, will be tangible and measurable as they will deal with basic skills and content.

FOUR BASIC ELEMENTS

An objective should contain the following four basic elements:

> *Who* is going to be acting?
>
> *What* action will take place?
>
> *When* will the action be performed?
>
> *How* will the action be measured?

Who

The first step in preparing an instructional objective is to specify who will be performing the desired behavior. Usually the term student is used in developing learning center objectives although terms such as *participant* and *learner* are also commonly used.

Example: After completing the activities in this center *students* will be able to list four essential components of learning centers, as determined by a written examination.

What

The second element in building an objective is to decide what it is a student should be able to do following completion of an action. When writing an objective that is behaviorally based, action verbs should be used. These verbs must be specifically related to the final desired and required action of the activity. Some of the action verbs most frequently used in writing objectives are the following:

apply	design	itemize	outline	solve
analyze	draw	interpret	paraphrase	specify
assemble	explain	judge	point out	summarize
build	extrapolate	list	predict	tell
change	find	locate	prepare	throw
clarify	formulate	make	produce	total
classify	graph	match	read	translate
count	hit	measure	recall	transfer
define	hold	name	report	use
demonstrate	identify	operate	restructure	write
describe	illustrate	organize	select	

Example: After completing the activities in this center, students will be able to *list* four essential components of learning centers, as determined by a written examination.

When

When developing a program of personalized instruction, time should not be more important than accomplishing objectives. Yet it may be important to specify a time limit within the objective to serve as a parameter or guideline. This helps many students to gauge the time to be spent on an activity. The teacher's professional experience can be called upon to place time parameters around an activity or assignment. Sometimes the time for an action will be specific to a particular day while, for others, expectations for completion will have greater latitude.

Example: *After completing the activities* in this center, students will be able to list four essential components of learning centers, as determined by a written examination.

How

Just as students must know what their goal is in a teaching-learning process, so must they know when they have reached it. The measurement of success, the final element in the preparation and use of objectives, is important to both teacher and learner. After a student has studied content at a center, it is imperative to provide feedback relative to degree of successful completion. Obviously the type of evaluative technique utilized will depend on the type of action performed. Some commonly used methods include teacher observations, worksheets, examinations, surveys, checklists, and teacher-student conferences.

Example: After completing the activities in this center, students will be able to list four essential components of learning centers, *as determined by a written examination.*

CONDENSED LISTS

Sometimes, depending on the ability level of your students, it is advantageous to post a condensed list of objectives on the center, as well as including highly specific ones. An objective is really only an intent. If teachers can get students excited about the content of a center, then maybe that is all that is needed to be accomplished for the moment. An example of a less sophisticated list of objectives might look like the following:

> At this center you can learn:
>
> 1. What learning centers are
>
> 2. How to use learning centers for:
>   a. regular study, single subject
>   b. enrichment
>   c. remedial work
>   d. independent study
>
> 3. Necessary components of a learning center
>
> 4. How to make a learning center
>
> 5. How to manage a learning center

A more specific list of objectives should be developed in addition to the above list and presented to students during their work at the center. These performance objectives might be contained in a folder located at the center or perhaps each activity card might state the specific objectives for which it was designed. Regardless of the ability level of the students, it is crucial to let them know the expected outcomes for which they will be held accountable.

The importance of stating objectives and presenting them to students cannot be overemphasized. Teachers do not have to get caught up in using educational jargon when writing objectives, and there is no mystique involved. Objectives are just simple statements, in precise language, that serve to guide and inform both student and teacher.

Directions

Directions for using a center are the second basic component of a successful center. A student should be able to go to a center and, by following clearly stated directions, initiate work and proceed through all the learning activities.

Generally, directions can serve two purposes: introducing the center and the activities to the student, and providing specific instructions on how to use the center from the beginning objective to the final activity. Because of the importance of this component, teachers frequently provide this information orally as well as posting it on the center. Obviously teachers want to avoid having students complete tasks that were never intended. This dilemma occurs all too frequently in schools, and the blame can usually be pointed at faulty or misleading direction-giving. If learning centers are to serve as self-contained learning units providing for individualized student study, the direction component cannot be slighted.

The following activity, designed to test both comprehension skills and physical reactions, underlines the importance of following directions. Before you do any further reading, find a soft lead pencil. Now, with pencil in hand, read the following directions and respond as quickly as you can. This activity should not take any longer than two minutes, so use your time accordingly. You may perform the tasks on this page.

1. Read everything before doing anything.
2. Write your name in the left margin of this page.
3. Circle the first direction.
4. Draw a rectangle around your name.
5. Put four stars on the top of your rectangle.
6. Below your name write "Yea!"
7. In the right margin of this page, divide 79,254 by 126.
8. Call out your answer to the above problem.
9. Add all the digits in your telephone number, including your area code. Use the right margin.
10. Call out your answer to problem nine.
11. Having read everything (as directed in direction one), do only direction two.

As you can see, directions, although seemingly explicit, can sometimes be just the contrary. Many students, upon reading the directions given, would charge ahead to complete extra tasks and then discover the error of their ways.

Frequently, just writing and posting directions is not enough. Field testing with a small group of students can serve as a good feedback device in discovering whether directions are adequate and doing the job as designed. Teacher observation and having students record their own progress on record sheets are two additional methods of obtaining evaluative data on the effectiveness and appropriateness of directions.

Activity Cards

Activity cards (sometimes referred to as task cards) are the third basic component and the heart of a center. Frequently, there are many activities that can be developed to accomplish a center's objectives. The more alternative activities a teacher can provide and the more choice a student is allowed in accomplishing an objective, the greater the probability of student success and achievement.

Activity cards serve as the device that links action (what will be performed at the center) to the appropriate objective. The cards provide detailed instructions related to work assigned, time allowed, materials needed, and what to do when the action is completed. Each card is designed to meet and satisfy an objective or objectives of the center. Quite often activity cards are sequential in nature and serve as building blocks, with each preceding piece of content requisite to each succeeding piece. Other activity cards might stand alone in achieving an objective and would not be dependent on previous or future learning.

Aesthetics

Although objectives, directions, and activity cards might seem the most important components of centers in the secondary school, the fourth component, aesthetics, is also of major significance. Color, design, and variety are all necessary ingredients in promoting motivation regardless of age or grade level. Well-developed objectives, directions, and activities will be of little use if a student is not "turned on" to using a center.

If they are to succeed as a teaching-learning tool, it is important to make centers as appealing to students as possible. Aesthetic details can often be the deciding factor in whether students will become excited about a particular area of study. It is not true that a center is a center is a center. The difference is often in how it appeals. Students like things to look at and a variety of activities to perform. A successful center will have color, games, charts, graphs, models, posters, pictures, resource materials, challenges— VARIETY.

It is sometimes easy to get carried away with the aesthetic side of building a learning center. For most teachers, this stage is a lot of fun. However, even though this component may be the deciding factor in arousing student interest in a center, it should not dominate a teacher's time. There are many time-saving ways to develop an attractive, motivating center. An overview of these ideas and materials is presented in Chapter five, "The Making of a Center."

A Sample Center

The following Learning Center on Learning Centers is designed to teach teachers, and it illustrates the four needed components: objectives, directions, activity cards, and aesthetics.

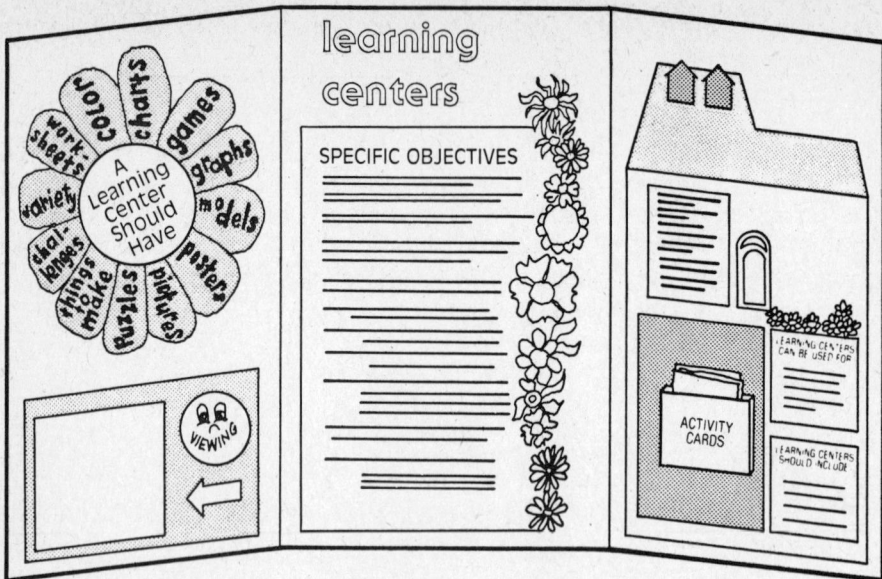

SPECIFIC OBJECTIVES OF THE SAMPLE CENTER

The specific objectives of the sample center are posted on the middle panel and state in performance terms just what students will be able to do after they have completed the activities.

SPECIFIC OBJECTIVES

After completing the activities in this center, students will be able to:

1. Define the term *learning center* as a teaching-learning concept.

2. Summarize the four basic uses of learning centers.

3. Explain the purpose of different sizes and shapes of learning centers and where they might be located in the classroom.

4. List and describe the four essential components of learning centers.

5. Write specific performance objectives in measurable terms.

6. List and describe the important elements in scheduling, managing, and evaluating a learning center.

7. Design, construct, implement, and manage a learning center.

DIRECTIONS FOR USING THE SAMPLE CENTER

Posted on the right wall of the sample center are the directions designed so that students will be able to begin and complete the program of study. Readability and clarity, combined with simplicity, are the qualities sought in these directions.

DIRECTIONS FOR USING THE LEARNING CENTER

1. Read the specific objectives posted on the middle panel of this center.

2. Study the section of the center captioned "A Learning Center Should Have . . ."

3. You are responsible for this center—keep it and all materials neat, clean, and orderly.

4. There are eight activity cards in this center. You can now begin with Activity Card #1.

THE ACTIVITY CARDS FOR THE SAMPLE CENTER

At the model learning center on learning centers, each activity card is sequential and follows the same order as this book does. The directions for completing each activity are presented on the appropriate card.

ACTIVITY CARD #1

1. Take the green folder entitled "Definition and Summary of Learning Centers" and read the enclosed paper. Do not write in this folder.

2. After reading the paper you should be able to respond to the following questions:
   a. What is a learning center?
   b. How does the learning center fit into the 1/3, 1/3, 1/3 curriculum approach?
   c. Why have learning centers been successful in both elementary and secondary classrooms?

3. Return the green folder and go on to Activity Card #2.

ACTIVITY CARD #2

1. View and listen to the slide/tape presentation "Learning Center Overview."

2. When you have finished, return the slides and tape to the center and disconnect all media equipment.

3. Go on to Activity Card #3.

ACTIVITY CARD #3

1. Read the paper in the blue folder entitled "Basic Uses of Learning Centers." Do not write in this folder. Be able to describe the following four types of centers.
   a. Single-subject
   b. Enrichment
   c. Remedial
   d. Independent-study

2. Take a sheet of paper and diagram your classroom including appropriate tables, desks, bulletin boards, chalk boards, sinks, etc. Assuming you desired to use the learning center approach in this classroom, what sizes and shapes of centers would you select and where would they be located? After you have decided, sketch the centers on your diagram.

3. Share your completed diagram with another teacher. Explain your decisions about center locations.

4. Return the blue folder and go on to Activity Card #4.

ACTIVITY CARD #4

1. Take several minutes and observe the learning center. Be particularly aware of the following four essential components:
   a. Specific objectives of the center
   b. Directions on how to use the center
   c. Activity cards to accomplish the center's objectives
   d. Aesthetics that attract and motivate

2. Take the red folder entitled "Things to Include in a Learning Center: Necessary Components" and read the enclosed paper. Do not write in the folder.

3. Be able to discuss the purpose of each of the above four components and to provide illustrations of each for a center designed for your classroom.

4. Return the red folder and go on to Activity Card #5.

ACTIVITY CARD #5

1. Take a copy of the paper "Objectives and How to Write Them." You may keep this paper.

2. After reading this paper, write three specific objectives with special attention given to the following four basic elements:
   a. *Who* is going to be acting?
   b. *What* action will take place?
   c. *When* will the action be performed?
   d. *How* will the action be measured?

3. Have the instructor review the three objectives you have written.

4. Go on to Activity Card #6.

ACTIVITY CARD #6

1. Take the orange folder entitled "Scheduling, Record-Keeping, and Evaluating Learning Centers." Read this paper but do not write in this folder.

2. Be able to discuss the following:
   a. The role of the student
   b. The role of the teacher
   c. Appropriate scheduling techniques for your situation
   d. Appropriate record keeping for your situation
   e. The importance of student assessment and feedback

3. Return the orange folder and go on to Activity Card #7.

ACTIVITY CARD #7

1. Look at the slides labeled "Elementary or Secondary" appropriate to your teaching level. These are examples of teacher-made centers covering each subject in the curriculum.

2. Examine several of the notebooks, developed by teachers, that contain descriptions and examples of the essential components of learning centers.

3. Examine several of the books on learning centers. Locate examples of centers that might be used in your classroom.

4. Return all materials to the center and go on to Activity Card #8.

ACTIVITY CARD #8

1. Select a single concept or skill in your subject area.

2. On a sheet of paper, sketch a three-panel center similar to the model, allowing room for objectives, directions, activity cards, and some aesthetic details.

3. Write one or two objectives for your selected subject.

4. Write two activities to meet each objective you have listed.

5. State the directions in sequential order so that a student will be able to complete all activities.

6. Add some color and design to your center so that it is appealing and motivating.

7. Give the completed sketch of your center to the instructor.

8. You have completed all of the objectives of this learning center and are ready to design, construct, and implement your personal teaching-learning centers.

THE AESTHETIC SIDE OF THE SAMPLE CENTER

The sample center on learning centers contains many of the aesthetic details that contribute to student motivation: color, variety, pictures, media presentations, resource materials, dittoes, and challenging activities.

Summary. This chapter has done the following:

1. Described and illustrated the four basic components of learning centers: objectives, directions, activity cards, and aesthetics.
2. Devoted special attention to how to write learning center objectives including the required elements of *who, what, when,* and *how.*
3. Presented an example of a learning center on learning centers that includes all four components.

THE MAKING OF A CENTER

Once a teacher has determined a center's educational mission and has spelled out the learning objectives, the directions on how to use the center, and the learning activities, it is time to construct the physical backdrop. How large or small a center should be is often a concern. The only correct answer to that question is that both size and shape are contingent upon the tasks involved and the classroom space available. Storage facilities should also be considered, although many centers are designed to collapse and therefore do not really require much space.

Chapter three provided a variety of examples of shapes and sizes of teacher-made centers. The most common shape of a center, however, has been the three-sided fold-a-way variety. This is a relatively simple center to make and it will be the model used in this chapter to describe the sequential steps in constructing a center. Other ideas and a list of materials are included which may inspire teachers to build original and unique centers.

Sequential Steps in Constructing a Center

Constructing a center is no more difficult than presented in the following six steps. As with most ventures, however, the first attempt always takes a little longer than subsequent ones. Once the techniques are mastered, production time is greatly reduced. Some secondary teachers have recruited student help in producing centers. For some students, the involvement provides an introduction to the class work to be accomplished. For others, it offers a means of working on an extra-credit project for reinforcement and retention purposes. Regardless of how many people are involved in construction, the process will remain the same.

Step 1: PLANNING BEFORE BUILDING

Most teachers draw the layout of their center prior to beginning construction. Graph paper is excellent to use as it provides an easy means of drawing

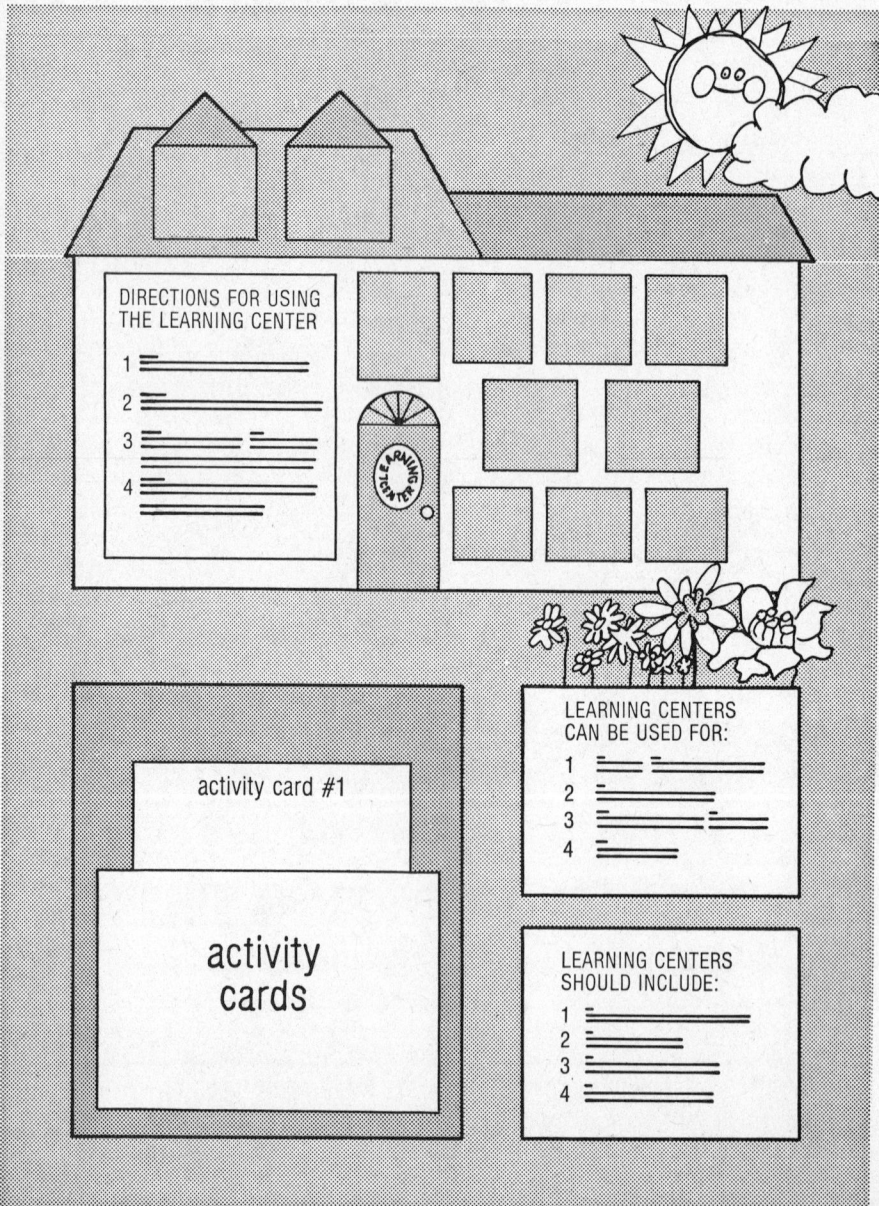

to scale. An example of the layout for one panel of the sample center described in Chapter four is presented here.

Many teachers prefer to just rough sketch their layout on a sheet of scratch paper prior to construction. Regardless of the sophistication of the preliminary drawing, it is important to plan before building.

Step 2: SELECTING A BACKDROP

A three-sided fold-a-way center usually has three panels of heavy-gauge cardboard as the backdrop. An easy way to obtain this durable cardboard is to make friends with a local appliance dealer. A mention that the discarded packing boxes will be used for educational purposes should be all that's needed to obtain whatever is necessary. The larger appliance boxes provide as big a panel of cardboard as teachers will ever want or need. A sharp cutting tool, perhaps even a small saw for heavy-duty jobs, is essential for cutting the boxes to the desired sizes.

Other types of materials that have served as backdrops for centers include pegboard, cork, acoustical ceiling panels, masonite, and pressed wood. When choosing materials, two important considerations need to be kept in mind.

1. Do not select material which is too heavy. Material must be relatively easy to work with and light enough to pick up and move for storing. Also, it should be easy to attach decorations and activity cards to this backdrop.

2. Do not select material which is too light in weight. Durability is important. Poster board and other light-gauge cardboard will not stand the weight of activity cards and other items posted on the center. They will soon warp and collapse.

Step 3: CUTTING BACKDROP PANELS

When cutting the panels for a three-sided center, two panels should be the same size, with the third panel being somewhat smaller in width.

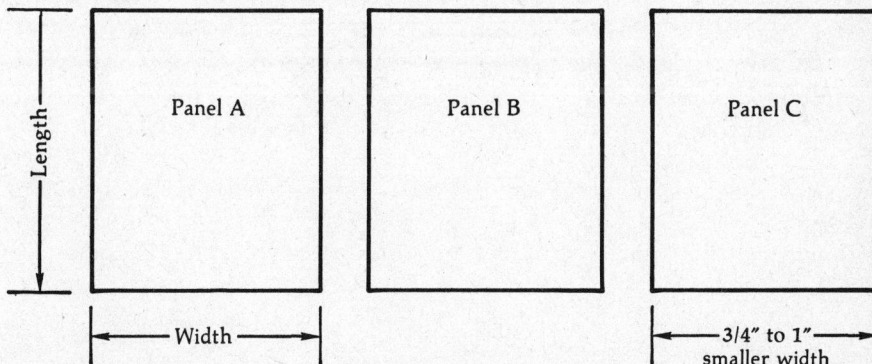

This is necessary if the center is to fold completely closed.

Step 4: COVERING THE BACKDROP

Unless a backdrop is already colorful and motivating, the panels should be covered with some attractive and eye-catching material. Everyone who makes a center seems to have a personal preference, although poster board, cloth, and contact paper rank high among materials used. Self-adhesive, plastic-coated shelf paper is a good choice because it is rapidly applied and provides good protection. It comes in various colors and designs, can be cleaned with a damp cloth, and is very durable. Cloth also comes in a variety of colors and designs, is easy and inexpensive to obtain, and can be attached to backdrops easily.

Poster board was the choice for our sample center, with each panel taking on a different color. Although poster board is plain, a multitude of bright and attractive colors are available. These can be decorated with additional cut-out materials if desired. Once attached, the poster board can be covered with clear contact paper or laminated for protection.

Be careful of using construction paper as it is very light-gauge paper and will tear easily. It also has a tendency to fade quickly.

Step 5: POSTING OBJECTIVES, DIRECTIONS, ACTIVITIES

When the backdrop is covered, the objectives of the center, directions on how to use it, and appropriate activity cards can be attached. Again, a good way to preserve these attached components is to laminate or use a clear contact paper. The clear contact paper is an inexpensive and easy way to keep materials clean and safe from tearing.

Step 6: TAPING THE PANELS

The final step in constructing the backdrop of a three-sided center is to connect the three panels. Although there are many types of tape that will work, teachers have found that cloth tape works the best. It does not stretch and should hold the center for as long as desired. Tape measuring 1-1/2 inches to 2 inches in width is most frequently used. This width is necessary because a gap of approximately 1/4 inch to 1/2 inch is needed between each of the three panels. (The thickness of the panels will decide the actual size of the gap.)

When the three panels are lined up, the smaller panel should be to one side. The gap (seam) between the panels should be taped both front and back. The tape will then serve as a hinge for smooth opening and closing.

Panel A   Panel B   Panel C

Seams 1/4" to 1/2"

Perimeter Taping

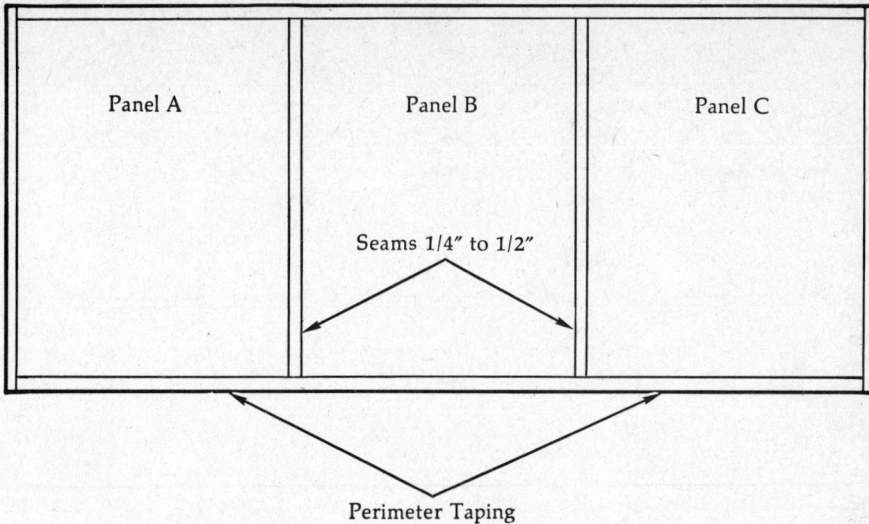

Many teachers complete their backdrop by taping the perimeter. This is particularly helpful if the panels have been covered with poster board or some other material where it is desirable that the edges be well protected.

OTHER IDEAS

Many secondary teachers have been innovative in the construction of their centers. The following suggestions are just a few of the possible variations that could be adapted for almost any classroom.

INDIVIDUAL STUDY CARRELS

Study carrels are excellent devices for providing individualized study areas. Although usually found in libraries and media centers, they are now being used by teachers in the regular classroom. The construction is rather

Panel A

Panel B

simple. By making a cut half-way through panels made of cardboard, ply-wood, cork, or pegboard, you can easily form study carrels. Once panels are joined to form a carrel, they are placed on tables for individual student study. Teachers have made four, six and even eight carrel areas.

(Slide the cut-a-way portions together to form four study carrels)

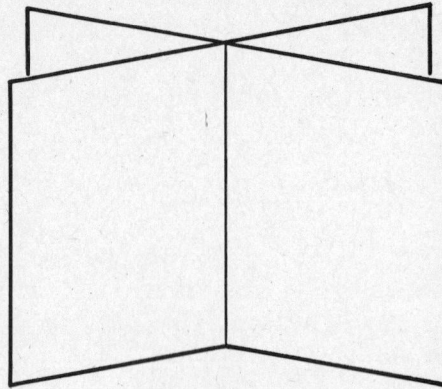

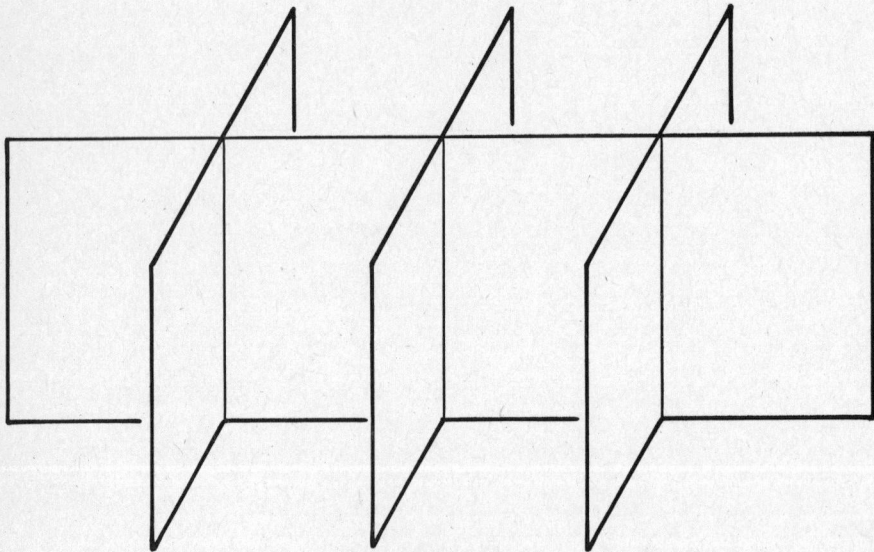

Four Study Carrels

Eight Study Carrels

USING A CUTTING BOARD

A cutting board or pattern board is usually known only to those who sew or cut out clothing. However, it is fast becoming a classroom item for those who want prefolded, ready-to-use learning center backdrops. A cutting board can be purchased that measures approximately 40 inches by 72 inches.

Cutting Board

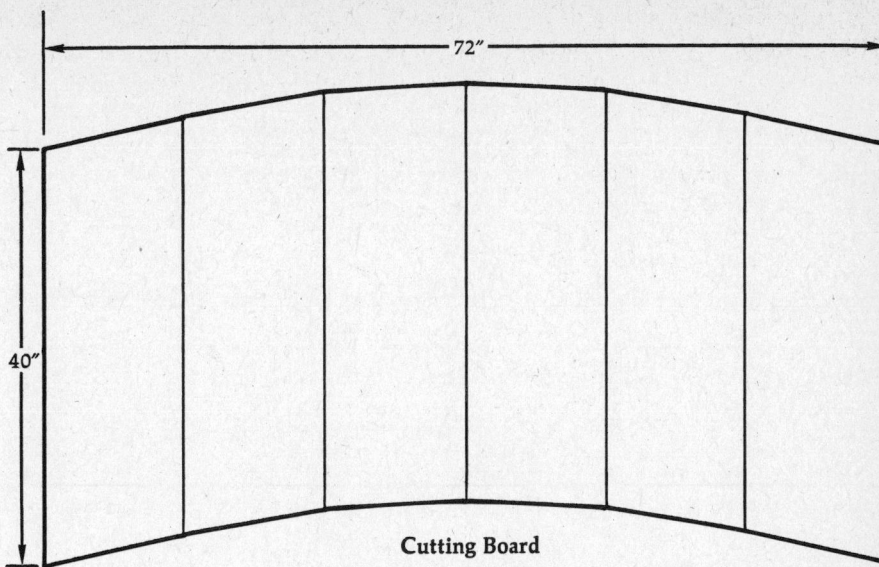

It can be used as one very large maxi-center, or it can be cut into two equal three-sided maxi-centers. If the mini-center approach is preferred, one cutting board can provide four conveniently sized three-sided mini-center backdrops each measuring 36 inches by 20 inches or six two-sided backdrops measuring 24 inches by 20 inches. Regardless of the size used, each backdrop is prefolded and ready to be covered.

Because it will be covered, an old board can also be used. Teachers can check out swap meets, garage sales, or even the family attic. The cost of a new board will also be fairly reasonable since it can be used for many centers.

GAME BOARDS

Game boards such as those used in Monopoly and checkers also provide good backdrop material. Such a board is automatically a prefolded two-sided mini-center ready to be covered. By adding a third panel, this can quickly be converted to a three-sided center. Most game boards are the same size and offer a quick and simple way to acquire classroom learning centers. Again, these can be found at garage sales, swap meets, or in family storage closets.

STORAGE BOXES

Teachers who use a lot of material at their centers have discovered that storage or packing boxes can serve their needs as learning centers. All materials are stored inside a box with the objectives, directions, and activity cards attached to the inside of the cover. The boxes used are usually shallow and storage is easy as they can be stacked one on the other. As with all centers, the tasks involved will dictate the size of the boxes needed.

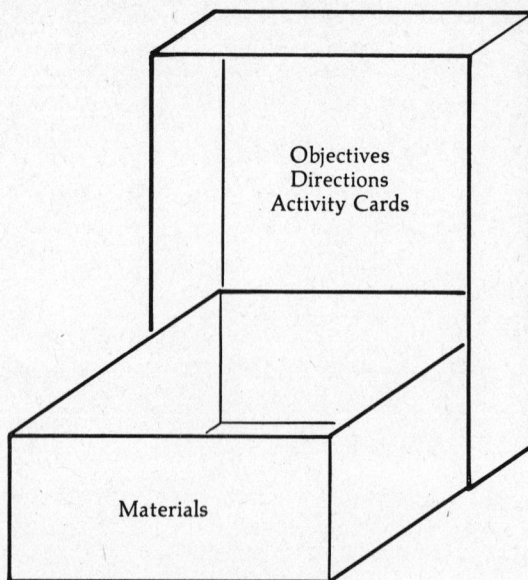

INTERCHANGEABLE PARTS

Because many teachers want to alternate or change the objectives, directions, and activity components of centers, without continuously constructing new and separate backdrops, interchangeable parts for learning centers are being used more and more. For example, panels of poster board can be designed and constructed that contain the necessary components for various areas of study. These can be attached to backdrops with clamps, paper clips, brads, glue, tacks, magnetic strips, or velcro and then removed and replaced by other panels as needed. This not only cuts down on expenses and construction time, but the panels require less storage space than complete centers when not in use.

DECORATING BACKDROPS

As mentioned in the previous chapter, well-developed objectives, directions, and activities will have little impact if a student does not "turn-on" to a center. The aesthetic side is very important as a motivator, yet teachers should not spend too much time on this component. The following ideas can help save time and still result in appealing centers. Many wallpaper stores will provide their outdated books of samples free of charge. Even without any artistic attributes, teachers can quickly cut out designs and patterns from these books to attach to center backdrops. Posters and gift-wrapping paper also produce artistic centers with the snip of a scissors. Once laminated or covered with clear contact paper, such backdrops become a permanent fixture that are easily cleaned and almost indestructible.

New and creative ideas continue to be generated as more and more teachers develop and experiment with learning centers. Some schools have set aside work areas for the development and construction of classroom instructional materials. With teachers sharing and contributing fresh ideas and materials, the adage "Your junk may be someone else's gold" often becomes a reality.

Tools, Equipment, and Materials

The following tools, equipment, and materials have been used in constructing learning centers. A glance at this list should help teachers generate ideas as they begin to design and construct learning centers.

bottles	felt pens	overhead	rubber tape
brads	felt strips	projector	ruler
burlap	file cards	packing boxes	scissors
cardboard	filmstrips	paint	scotch tape
chalk	glue	paint brushes	slide projector
clamps	glue magnets	paper clips	slide sorter
clay	glue sticks	paper cutter	slides
clothes pins	gummed labels	paper punch	sponges
colored pencils	gummed	paste	stapler
colored string	reinforcements	pegboard	staples
colored yarn	hammer	pens	stencil
compass	index cards	photographs	stick-on
construction paper	laminating material	pieces of cloth	decorations
contact paper,	lettering materials	pins	tape recorder
clear	magazines	pipe cleaners	thumb tacks
contact paper,	magnetic strips	plastic bag ties	tin cans
patterned	manila folders	plastic bags	transparencies
copy machine	masking tape	plastic folders	typewriter
cork	metal (or plastic)	post cards	velcro
corner rounder	spinners	poster board	vinyl letters
crayons	mirror-mounting	razor blades	wallpaper
cut-out letters	squares	ribbon	yardstick
duct tape	nails or screws	rope	x-acto knife
envelopes	opaque projector	rubber bands	

Summary. This chapter has done the following:

1. Described the sequential steps to be followed when constructing a learning center:
   a. Planning before building
   b. Selecting a backdrop
   c. Cutting backdrop panels
   d. Covering the backdrop
   e. Posting objectives, directions, activities
   f. Taping the panels
2. Provided some creative and time-saving ideas which have been developed by classroom teachers
3. Presented a list of tools, equipment, and materials used in the development and construction of centers

6

SCHEDULING, RECORD KEEPING, AND EVALUATION

In day-to-day life many people become bound by traditional ways of doing things, and afraid to try anything new because it would be too disruptive, too great a change. This is often true in the world of education as well. However, teachers needn't be concerned that the adoption of learning centers will force a total revamping of their learning programs. Teachers do not need to redesign the entire curriculum or change their expectations for student achievement. What is really being done in the adoption of the learning center approach is repackaging a portion of the course curriculum to fit a new instructional mode. The same instructional objectives, the same activities and experiences, and the same quizzes and final examinations can still be used, but on an individualized basis. Change is necessary only if deemed important by each teacher. The housekeeping chores of scheduling, record keeping, and evaluation that are involved in implementing centers may be slightly different than with a regular program but any problems this causes can easily be worked out through experience.

Scheduling

There is no one way to introduce learning centers to the classroom initially. Both informal, unannounced beginnings and more formal introductions have proved successful.

For example, one high school English teacher's first attempt at utilizing a learning center dealt with grammar, so he decided not to frighten any potential users by formally introducing it to the class. Rather he selected a corner to set up the center and casually continued with the normal classroom routine. Much to his surprise students began to gather around the center at the beginning and end of the class periods. Several asked to go to the center when they had some free time. A colorful center with interesting activities had evoked interest despite its topic.

A second method employed to introduce centers is one that is more conventional in nature and one that has been extremely effective. Once a center is ready for classroom use, it is introduced to the class as a whole through an oral presentation by the teacher. Often students will raise common concerns and questions, which can be responded to and answered at one time. This provides for a smooth implementation as each factor (objectives, directions, activities, materials and evaluation) can be discussed.

Once the center has been introduced, the type of learning center will obviously dictate the way the teacher will schedule its use. For example, centers designed for remedial work, enrichment, or independent study will not involve every student in the class. Because only a limited number of students use these types of centers, scheduling is relatively simple. A single-subject center, however, is frequently designed to be used by each student in a class. The scheduling for this type of center is more difficult, particularly if there is only one center in the classroom. Yet, one center designed to teach a single-subject skill or concept can be used with great success.

For example, one English teacher began using learning centers by designing and constructing a single-subject center to teach writing skills to thirty-nine tenth-grade students. The students first drew slips of colored paper to form three student groups. Each group was then scheduled into the center to work individually on specific writing skills activities. A follow-up survey revealed no decline in learning achievement as compared to the more conventional teaching-learning pattern of large-group instruction. More importantly, students expressed renewed interest and enthusiasm toward learning.

In order to achieve such a success with centers, the teacher must allow individualization to take place. Adoption of the 1/3, 1/3, 1/3 teaching-learning concept, or some similar approach that provides time to individualize instruction, is the first major decision that must be made.* Time must be set aside for it if individualized learning is desired.

There are no cookbook recipes as to how to work out a specific schedule for the use of centers in a classroom. Too many variables enter into the scheme of things: time factors, the number of centers available, types of centers, numbers of students, subjects, and difficulty and length of objectives and activities. The best thing to do at the start is to experiment with

---

*A complete description of the 1/3, 1/3, 1/3 approach is presented in Chapter two.

methods that seem appropriate to the classroom situation. The teacher might be the sole decision maker and assign students to centers. On the other hand, students might sign up for centers depending on their personal interests and learning needs. A third method might be for the teacher to hold a conference with each student and together they can decide on how and when to schedule center time.

For those who are using learning centers for the first time, the most important advice is to *go slowly*. Introduce the center completely, explaining how it is to be used. Clarify the specific directions, activities, and evaluation/ feedback components. Discuss all aspects with the students. Each teacher will soon get a "feel" for using centers. Easing into the concept, coupled with having specific requirements and expectations, will pay large dividends.

Record Keeping

Record keeping is usually not much fun but it doesn't necessarily have to be a headache. Its importance is evident in that it provides an account of who has used a center, what activities/objectives have been attempted, and the degree of achievement. This information is important to the student and teacher in the classroom along with providing parents with a description of both success and failure.

Many teachers feel that the easiest way to keep records is to develop a file with an individual folder for each student. Usually this is a typical manila folder with the student's name at the top for easy reference. All work completed at a center is kept in the folder for safekeeping and future reference. When new activities are completed, the folder is placed in a special location so the teacher can evaluate the work and provide feedback. Following assessment, the folder is again placed in a central filing area.

Besides the completed work, each folder can contain a record sheet that includes such information as a listing of objectives, activities, and evaluative information regarding student participation at the center. As a student completes an activity, this is recorded on the record sheet. When all the center activities have been completed and evaluated, the teacher can pull the record sheet to keep as a permanent record, leave it in the folder for future student use, or send it home to the parents as an information sheet of student accomplishment. Record sheets are usually put on dittoes so that multiple copies can be made. They can take many forms and the following is provided as only one model.

The folder system has proven to be successful for various reasons. It provides a confidentiality factor which is important to most students. It also provides a storage area for various worksheets and assignments that are a part of the center activities, and it allows for an easy "in-basket/out-basket" approach for teachers to evaluate progress and to provide constructive feedback. However, the same basic information can also be recorded and

---

LEARNING CENTER RECORD SHEET

Student Name: _____

Class Period: _____

Name of Center: _____

Center Activities	"X" Box When Completed	Date Completed	Teacher Assessment/ Comment
1. _____	☐	_____	_____
2. _____	☐	_____	_____
3. _____	☐	_____	_____
4. _____	☐	_____	_____
5. _____	☐	_____	_____

Final Teacher Comments: _____
_____
_____

Final Evaluation: _____

---

stored on file cards or some sort of master chart. Each method could utilize an alphabetical index and could be divided by class section or by the specific group of students who would be using a particular center. Some teachers have color-coded folders, file cards, *and* charts to distinguish various classes or to set apart different learning centers.

An important thing to remember, along with the advice presented previously of "going slowly," is to keep the operation of centers simple. Don't get overwhelmed by a lot of paperwork, in terms of grading and record keeping. Allow students to participate in all areas of the program including record keeping and evaluation. Part of the success of any program is related to having students and teachers share responsibility.

Evaluation

Although evaluation is usually considered the end of a learning program, it can also be the beginning. When learning centers are utilized, a preassessment program is often used to diagnose the ability and achievement level needs of students. This, by its very nature, puts evaluation as the first step in the teaching-learning process. Evaluation also becomes the culminating step as a student's accomplishments are reviewed in terms of some norm. This criterion could be determined from standardized data or in terms of individual student growth. Much of the difficulty in the task of evaluating is eliminated if the specific learning objectives to be accomplished have been clearly stated. This can simplify and hasten the task of appraising completed work.

Once evaluation is completed and duly recorded (for example, on a student record sheet), the data should be used to reinforce and enhance the learning that has occured. A successful and proven method is to schedule regular teacher-student conferences. Another excellent communication channel is the parent-student-teacher conference. Each type of conference can create positive conditions for all participants relative to activities that occur both in and out of school.

A simplified schematic model for evaluation and feedback follows:

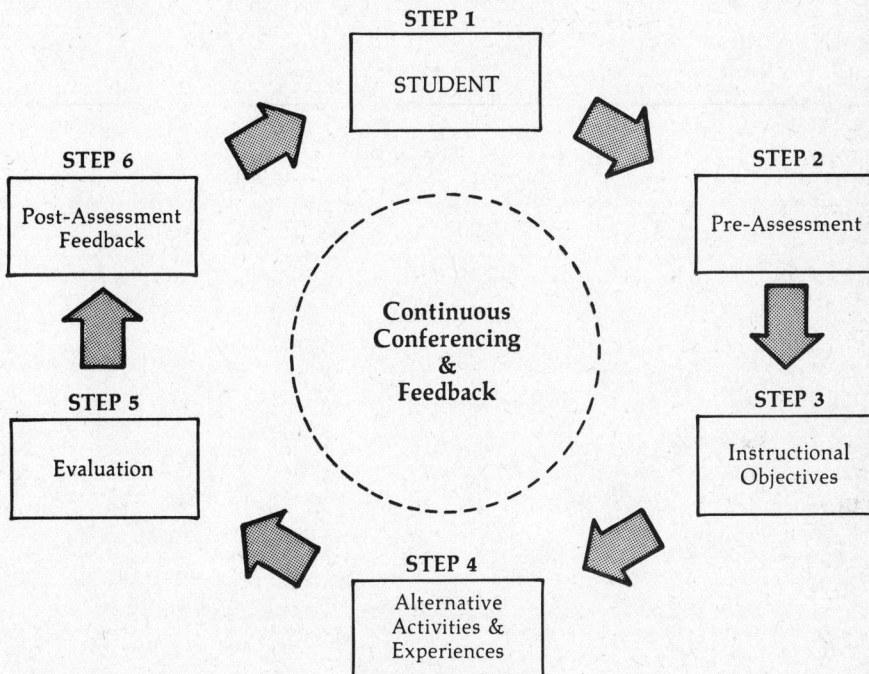

The model is simplified so that a perspective of the cyclical process can be gained. In reality, evaluative assessment and feedback is a continuous process. Periodic student self-assessment, together with constant teacher assessment, provides the best conditions for student growth and achievement.

Summary. This chapter has done the following:

1. Presented two methods of introducing learning centers to the classroom
2. Discussed the factors that influence scheduling of center use and introduced some possible methods of scheduling
3. Described the individual-folder method of record keeping
4. Provided an evaluation-feedback model

PART TWO

A Curriculum Overview: Examples of Centers That Work

ENGLISH/LANGUAGE ARTS •

MATHEMATICS •

SCIENCE •

SOCIAL STUDIES •

ART •

BUSINESS EDUCATION •

CONSUMER AND FAMILY STUDIES •

FOREIGN LANGUAGE •

HEALTH AND SAFETY •

INDUSTRIAL EDUCATION •

MUSIC •

PHYSICAL EDUCATION •

SPECIAL EDUCATION/ LEARNING ASSISTANCE •

Learning centers come in many shapes and sizes, and can be used in a variety of ways to teach any subject in the secondary school curricula. To help teachers develop appropriate centers for their classrooms, this part of the book is devoted to providing concrete, teacher-made, field-tested examples.

The centers provided can be replicated, or serve as springboards to developing approaches that more closely meet personal teaching-learning needs. Some are devoted to basic skills, while others stress the development of creative thought. Examples of single-subject, enrichment, remedial, and independent-study centers are provided. Each sample contains a statement of specific objectives, and one or more activity cards. Some examples are illustrated and contain a list of directions. The teacher can create a personal tone by directly addressing the student, or a more objective one by using "the student" or "the participant" in the text. The following sample centers give you an example of both. Although not all the subject areas will be directly relevant to all teachers, those learning centers that fall outside one's personal teaching area, if utilized as an idea springboard, can conjure notions leading to the development of centers within the appropriate subject or to those having an interdisciplinary appeal.

track it down
(Developing Library Research and Dictionary Skills)

STUDENT OBJECTIVES

After working at this center, the student will be able to:

1. Use reference sources such as almanacs, reader's guides, encyclopedias, and the card catalog to locate information
2. Perform basic dictionary skills such as syllabication, pronunciation, spelling, and plurals
3. Locate books on library shelves by using the Dewey Decimal System

DIRECTIONS TO FOLLOW

1. Observe the center; note its parts and arrangement.
2. Select an area of concentration—either *Library Research* or *Dictionary Skills*.
3. Complete the activities described on the appropriate Activity cards.
4. Work individually unless an Activity card specifies more than one person. (No more than three persons can work at the center at one time.)

DIRECTIONS (continued)

5. Keep the center neat and orderly.
   Replace Activity cards when finished
   and do not write on them or any other
   part of the center.
6. Turn in completed work to the teacher.

SAMPLE ACTIVITY CARDS

Using Abbreviations

After referring to the "Key to Abbreviations" and to the "Lists of Periodicals Indexed" at the front of the *Reader's Guide*, give the meaning of each of the following:

1. Sci N.L.
2. COND
3. 54: 320-56
4. ATLAN
5. v
6. Je
7. SCH & SOC
8. ABR
9. +
10. por

The Dewey Decimal System

Take the worksheet entitled "Cracking Dewey's Code." Using the card catalog, write down the call number and the category of each of the listed titles.

Syllabication

List your current vocabulary words. Using the dictionary as your source, divide them into syllables and accent the correct syllable(s).

I'm a poet 'n I know it

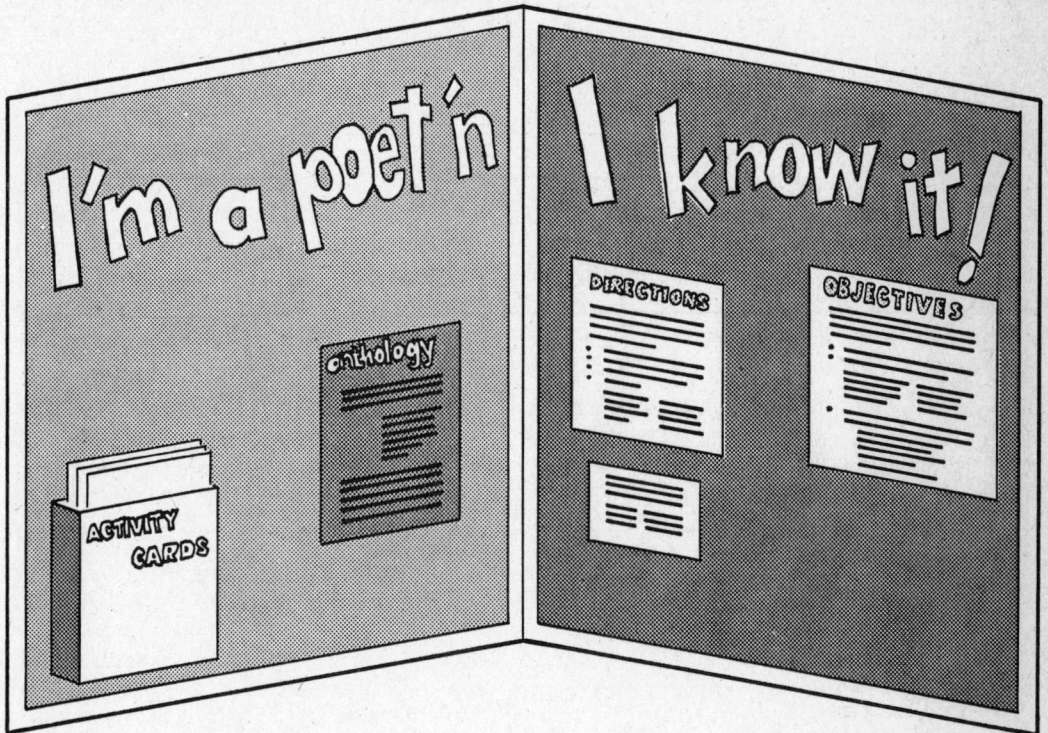

STUDENT OBJECTIVES

After working at this learning center, you will be able to:

1. Compile a personal anthology of creative poetry
2. Write each of the following kinds of poems:
   a. Haiku
   b. Story poem
   c. Limerick
   d. Shape poem
   e. Cinquain
   f. A poem containing a simile
   g. A poem containing a metaphor
   h. A sound poem containing alliteration
   i. A sound poem containing onomatopoeia
3. Write at least three of the following kinds of poems:
   a. A one-sentence poem
   b. A color poem
   c. An "I Wish" poem

OBJECTIVES (continued)

d. An "I Used To Be, But Now . . ." poem
e. A crossword poem
f. A five-sense poem
g. A septone
h. A four-word poem
i. A found poem

DIRECTIONS TO FOLLOW

1. Before an anthology is compiled, the work for each activity card should be done on a separate piece of paper and checked by the teacher.
2. All work should be in cursive!
3. When you complete the work for each activity card, put your name, the date, and the card number in the upper right-hand corner. Place finished work in the basket in the center.
4. Remember to return each activity card to the center when you are through with it.
5. Nine of the activity cards are marked "required." You must do all of them.
6. You may choose any three of the remaining nine activity cards—the rest of the cards are optional.
7. After doing all of the required activity cards, and those optional cards selected, put your anthology together as follows:
   a. Make attractive front and back covers using construction paper provided in the center, or any material you would like to supply.
   b. Create a title page.
   c. Rewrite each poem to be included on a page by itself, after it has been checked by your teacher. Each poem should have a title, which should be neatly handwritten. (When you have written more than one poem of a kind, choose your favorite example to include.)
   d. Number all pages in your anthology, putting numbers in the center of the bottom of each page.
   e. Assemble all the material in the proper order and secure with brads or other appropriate fasteners.

SAMPLE ACTIVITY CARD

One-Sentence Poems

A one-sentence poem is actually one sentence put into five lines.

1st line—Identify something—an object, person, feeling.
2nd line—Use descriptive words to describe what is in the line one.
3rd line—Provide more details about the description given in line two.
4th line—Use additional descriptive words.
5th line—End your sentence.

Example #1

My rusty skateboard sits
Waiting to blitz down the sidewalk,
Splitting the air with speed,
Zooming down the ramp,
A modern day chariot.

Example #2

The swaying trees bend
Loving the wind,
Caressing the breeze,
Clutching the rustling
Close to its side.

YOUR TASK: Write several one-sentence poems. Try one on a topic that is *not* your favorite subject to see how it sounds. Remember to use separate sheets of paper for your work and to put completed poems in the basket at the center.

the world of Shakespeare
(Some Background Information)

STUDENT OBJECTIVES

After working at this center, the student will be able to:

1. Demonstrate acquaintance with certain of Shakespeare's plays
2. Show an understanding of the facets of drama
3. Develop competence in the interpretation of literature
4. Show awareness of the intricacies of plot, character, and theme
5. Discuss the "living" Shakespeare as well as the man of the Elizabethan Era
6. Connect the common vision of our humanity and the human predicament to the work of Shakespeare
7. Show improvement in the understanding and use of language
8. Exhibit skills in various forms of composition
9. Use a wider vocabulary

SAMPLE ACTIVITY CARD

Introductory Information

Select any one of the three options provided below.

1. Research the subject *Shakespeare's England*, and then write a short essay on one of the following topics: family life, London, religion, royalty, plague, sanitation, crime and punishment, war, or education.

2. Discover what the theatre was like in Shakespeare's time. Based on your research, write a short essay on one of the following topics: location, public attitude, or physical structure.
3. Read some material concerning Shakespeare's life. Based on what you have learned, write a short essay on one of the following topics: parents, social position, marriage, children, occupations, or how people reacted to him.

synonyms, antonyms, and homonyms
(Increasing Vocabulary)

STUDENT OBJECTIVES

After working at this center, the student will be able to:

1. Define and give examples of synonyms
2. Define and give examples of antonyms
3. Define and give examples of homonyms

4. Demonstrate use of a thesaurus
5. Review the basic parts of speech
6. Exhibit creativity in word choice
7. Use an increased vocabulary

SAMPLE ACTIVITY CARD

Using the Thesaurus

Find the word *hindrance* in *Roget's Thesaurus* and do the following on a 5 x 8 card:

1. Write four synonyms for this word that you can use comfortably.
2. Locate the antonym for *hindrance* in the thesaurus and write four synonyms that can be used in its place.
3. Write sentences using all of the words that you've written down. (You may use more than one of the words in each sentence if desired.)

Rx for better punctuation

STUDENT OBJECTIVES

When you finish the activities at this center, you will be able to:

1. Match the name of each punctuation mark with its symbol
2. Recognize if a sentence is correctly punctuated or not
3. Change the meaning of a sentence by changing the punctuation
4. Take an unpunctuated paragraph and punctuate it appropriately so that its meaning is clear

SAMPLE ACTIVITY CARD

Punctuation Symbols

1. Take a copy of the worksheet called "Punctuation Symbols."
2. Write the corresponding punctuation symbol beside each word. Use the space provided. (If necessary, the resource material in the center can be consulted.)

Worksheet
Punctuation Symbols

_____ 1. Comma	_____ 7. Semi-colon
_____ 2. Apostrophe	_____ 8. Exclamation point
_____ 3. Period	_____ 9. Quotation marks
_____ 4. Colon	_____ 10. Parentheses
_____ 5. Question mark	_____ 11. Hyphen
_____ 6. Dash	_____ 12. Brackets

focus on writing
(Mastering Written Communication)

STUDENT OBJECTIVES

Upon completion of the activities in this center, you will be able to:

1. Write a topic sentence
2. Write a paragraph of about six sentences containing a topic sentence and supporting details
3. Write a concluding sentence for a paragraph
4. Formulate a thesis
5. Write a four-paragraph composition with a thesis
6. Use transitions smoothly
7. Write a five-paragraph essay with a thesis and an argument refuting the thesis

SAMPLE ACTIVITY CARD

Transitional Words and Phrases

In a good paragraph the thought flows easily from sentence to sentence. Transitional elements help build bridges from one sentence to the next, and help make the organization of the paragraph clear to the reader. The following are only a few of the many words and phrases that can be used.

actually	finally	otherwise
after a short while	hence	then
after that	however	therefore
also	indeed	thus
and, but, or	in fact	to begin with
as a matter of fact	meanwhile	while
as a result	nevertheless	whenever
because of	now	yet
consequently	on the other hand	

YOUR TASK: 1. On the front page of today's newspaper, select a story and underline in red each transitional word you can find.
2. Read over the four-paragraph composition you wrote at this center and underline the transitional words you used.

how do you measure up?

(A Metric Approach)

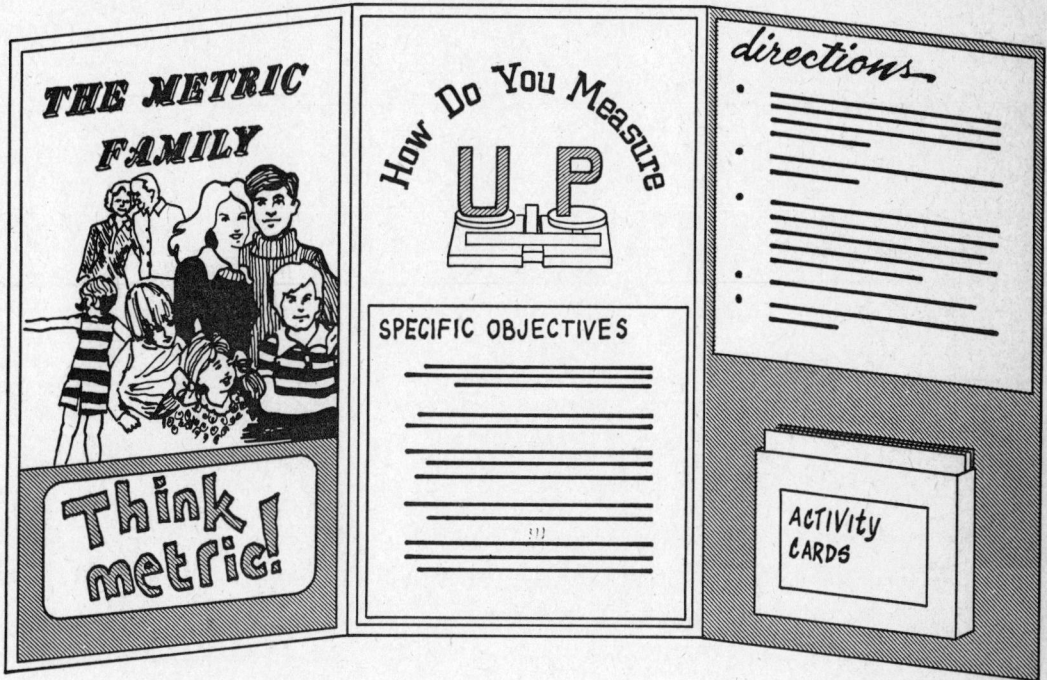

STUDENT OBJECTIVES

After completing the activities in this center, the student will be able to:

1. Measure linear distance, volume, and mass, using the appropriate metric categories of meter, liter, and gram
2. Select the appropriate metric prefix to indicate the quantity of meter, liter, or gram, to be measured, from the following list: kilo-, centi-, milli-, and micro-
3. Use the metric ruler to accurately determine the linear dimensions of unknown materials to the nearest 1.0 millimeter
4. Use the graduated cylinder to accurately determine the volume of an unknown liquid to the nearest 0.2 milliliter
5. Use the laboratory balance to accurately weigh unknown materials to the nearest 0.01 gram
6. Choose an appropriate metric unit that closely approximates a given English measurement (such as quart and liter)

OBJECTIVES (continued)

7. Convert between the English and metric systems of measurement

DIRECTIONS TO FOLLOW

1. Complete all activity cards in order.
2. Complete all worksheets as indicated on the activity cards.
3. Be sure the center is clean and neat before you leave it.
4. Follow all instructions and *have fun!!!*

SAMPLE ACTIVITY CARD

Measuring Volume

1. During this activity, you will be measuring volume. First, find two tall cylindrical glasses, (called graduated cylinders) located on the learning center table in front of you.
2. Take a copy of the worksheet titled "Learning to Measure Metrically" and begin this activity with Item #1.
3. Write all answers on the worksheet, and, when it is completed, have the teacher check it before you proceed to the next activity card.

Worksheet
Learning to Measure Metrically

1. You should have found two sizes of graduated cylinders, one big and one small. Fill each about ½ full of water.

2. Look very closely at the water level. See how it bends? This is called a *meniscus*. Use the bottom of the meniscus to determine the exact water level in the graduated cylinder.

3. What are the units marked on the sides of the cylinders? _____.

   What is the basic unit of metric volume? _____ . How many

   milliliters are there in 1 liter? _____ .

---

4. How many mLs will the small graduated cylinder hold? _____.

   How many will the large one hold? _____. This maximum level
   is called the *capacity*.

5. Read and record below, the water levels in the two graduated cylinders to
   the nearest 0.1 mL.

   a. small cylinder =

   b. large cylinder =

line design meets string art

(Geometric Patterns)

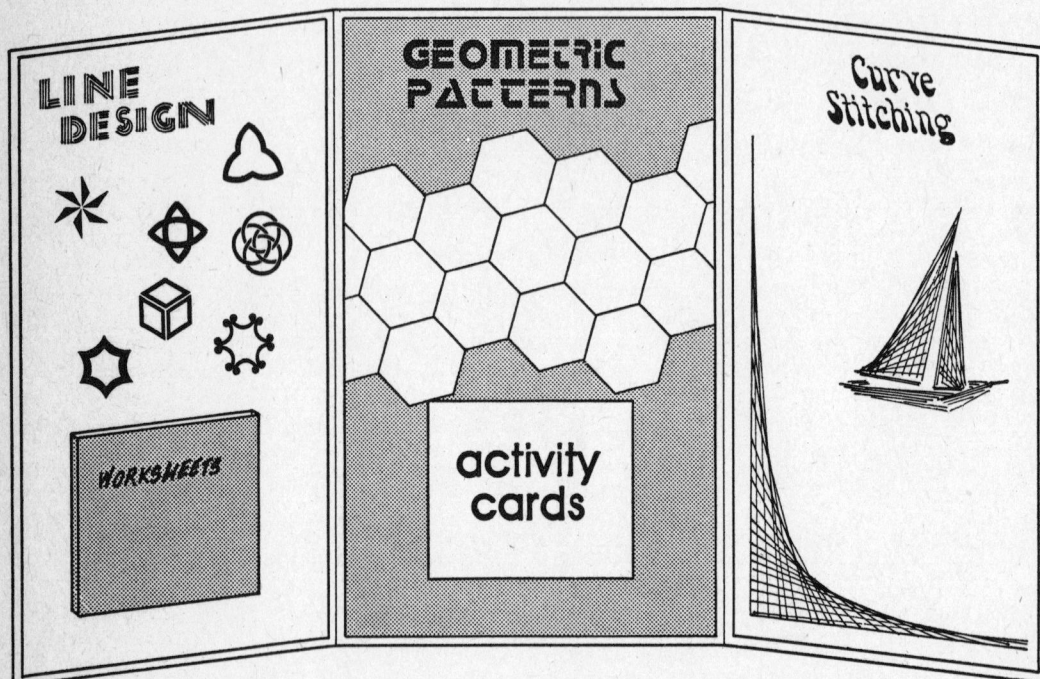

STUDENT OBJECTIVES

At this center you will be able to:

1. Plan and draw geometric patterns using the basic line-design technique
2. Plan and produce geometric patterns using the basic technique of curve stitching
3. Have fun with math

DIRECTIONS TO FOLLOW

There are six activity cards and one introductory worksheet for this center. Begin by reading and following all directions on the worksheet entitled "Line Design." Then do all of the activity cards in numerical order. Have fun!

SAMPLE ACTIVITY CARDS

Drawing Line Designs

This activity will show you how to make beautiful geometric curves (line designs) by drawing a series of straight lines.

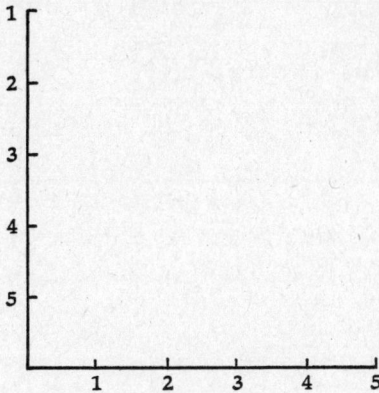

A. In the figure above, connect like numbers (1 to 1, 2 to 2, etc.) with a straight edge.

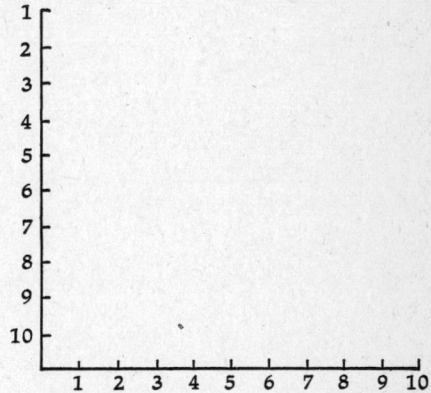

B. Notice the curve that was formed in figure A. Connect the like numbers above and notice the difference in the design when the equal parts are closer together.

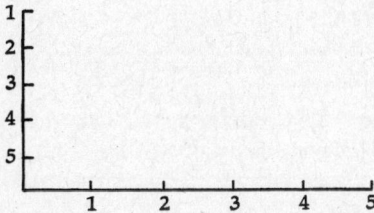

C. The two sides of the angle do not need to be equal in length. However, they do need to be divided into the same number of parts. Connect the like numbers above to see the effect.

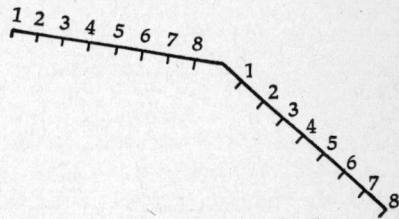

D. The angle for the line design need not be a right angle. Connect the like numbers of the angle above to see the effect.

Worksheet
Line Design

Line designs are geometric patterns formed entirely by the use of straight lines that produce the illusion of a curve. When first seeing one of the designs you will have to look closely to convince yourself that no curved lines are used. This interesting property produces fascinating results, yet line designs are relatively simple to do.

Line designs are formed by connecting certain sequences of points with line segments. Different designs are formed by selecting points in various ways. The most common way is to connect equally spaced points along the two sides of an angle as shown and described below.

1. Draw an angle with two sides of the same length.
2. Divide each side into an equal number of segments and mark as shown.
3. Connect point 1 with point 1, point 2 with point 2, and so on until all the points are connected.

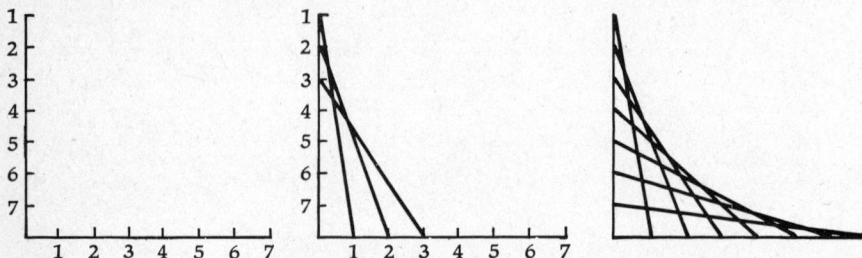

A greater number of divisions on the side of an angle will result in a design which is more dense. The sides of the angle need not be the same length. However, divide each side into the same number of equal parts.

You can combine two or more angles to make a variety of designs, but always use the basic line-design technique.

the Pythagorean theorem

STUDENT OBJECTIVES

By working at this center, the student will:

1. Develop an understanding of the basic structure of algebra as a foundation for advanced study

2. Acquire facility in applying algebraic concepts and skills

3. Extend the ability to reason abstractly

4. Build a mathematical vocabulary used in deductive reasoning

SAMPLE ACTIVITY CARD

Right Triangles

From the box on the table, take the envelope marked "Blocks." Now do the following:

1. Placing the blocks side by side, form a right triangle.

   Example:

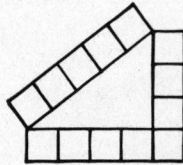

   (However, use more than three blocks for your altitude and four blocks for your base.)

2. On a separate sheet of paper, write the number of blocks you have for:

   Hypotenuse _____

   Altitude _____

   Base _____

3. On this same piece of paper, substitute your answers for question two above in the formula:

   $$c^2 = a^2 + b^2$$

4. Write a postulate of one or more sentences as a result of your experimentation.

5. When you have completed all of the above, read the evaluation sheet that corresponds to this activity card.

calculating numbers
(Learning Basic Number Facts)

STUDENT OBJECTIVES

The user of this center will be able to:

1. Become a wise consumer
2. Perform basic number operations in addition, subtraction, multiplication, and division
3. Use the mini-calculator as a practical and instructional aid

SAMPLE ACTIVITY CARDS

Let's Calculate

YOUR TASK: 1. Turn on the calculator at the center.

2. Clear all entries.

3. Add: $5 + 5 =$
             $9 + 35 + 268 + 1470 =$

4. Subtract: $10 - 5 =$
             $1492 - 687 =$
             $(380 + 475) - 534 =$

5. Multiply: $2 \times 5 =$
             $284 \times 16 =$
             $(1485 + 508 - 613) \times 8 =$

6. Divide: $10 \div 2 =$
             $568 \div 35 =$
             $[(1748 + 1634 - 2280) \times 23] \div 14 =$

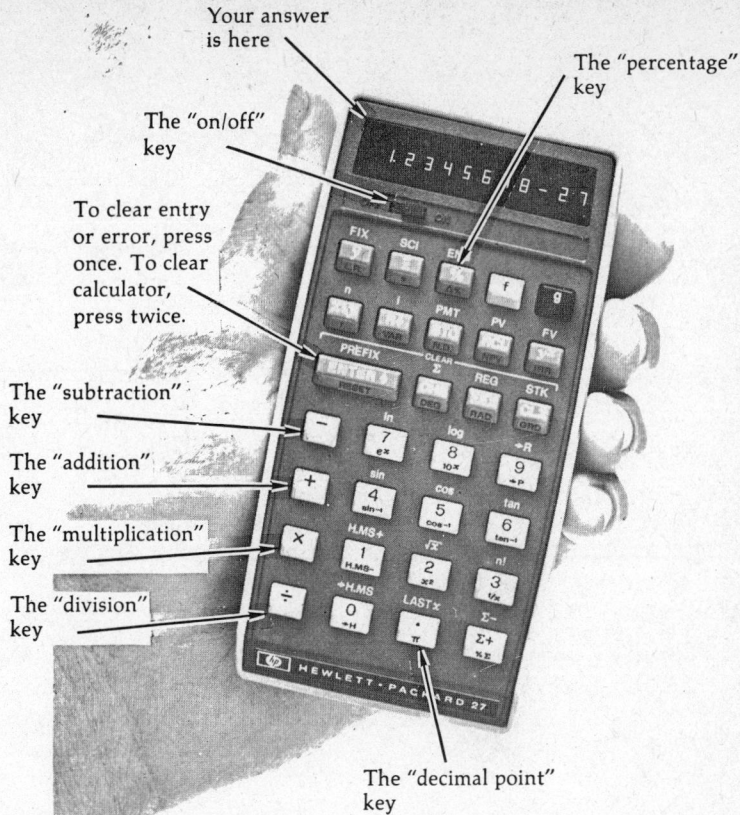

Your answer is here

The "percentage" key

The "on/off" key

To clear entry or error, press once. To clear calculator, press twice.

The "subtraction" key

The "addition" key

The "multiplication" key

The "division" key

The "decimal point" key

Photo courtesy of the Hewlett-Packard Company

Worksheet
Multiple Madness

You have just invested $125.00 in a calculator company. Your investment is to double every two years. If this occurs, what will your investment be in:

2 years? _____   14 years? _____

4 years? _____   20 years? _____

8 years? _____

Write your answers on the answer sheets provided.

checks and balances

STUDENT OBJECTIVES

At this center you can learn to:

1. Shop and save money

2. Compute sales tax
3. Balance a checkbook

SAMPLE ACTIVITY CARDS

Making a Checkbook

1. Make a checkbook like the sample by cutting thirty checks and six deposit slips from the activity sheets located at the center. Use construction paper for the checkbook cover and fasten with the book tape and staples.
2. Study the sample checkbook until you feel confident you can write a check properly.

Shopping for Groceries

1. Compile a list of fifteen food items that you wish to purchase.
2. Using a newspaper advertisement or a trip to the store as your source, write a price for each item on the list.
3. Add the total cost of these products and write a check to cover this expense.
4. Starting with a balance of $500.00 in your checking account, subtract the check covering the cost of the groceries.

Get the Most for Your Money

Using a department store catalog, compile a list of items that you could purchase for exactly $100.00, including a 6 percent sales tax. See how many bargains you can find, and how much you can buy for your $100.00. Give the name of the store and list the items by name and cost.

Example: Sears

Tool Chest	$ 19.95
Saw	9.40
Screw driver set	5.65
Hammer	7.95
Electric drill	32.50
Sandpaper	.54
Level	8.50
Chisel Set	9.85

Total		$ 94.34
Sales tax	×	.06
		$5.6604
Items	=	$ 94.34
Sales tax	=	5.66
		$100.00

wildlife needs you!

WILDLIFE NEEDS YOU

ACTIVITY CARDS

OBJECTIVES

STUDENT OBJECTIVES

After completing the activities in this learning center, the student will be able to:

1. List at least ten endangered species and describe why some of them are truly endangered
2. Describe the problems of protecting wildlife and cite several specific ways to do so
3. Locate major magazines and resources related to wildlife for future reference
4. List several wildlife management techniques and discuss their relative success

5. Describe the state's role in protecting wildlife

DIRECTIONS TO FOLLOW

1. There are only three activity cards for this center. However, there are a variety of projects on each card for you to do.
2. Have fun with this center but keep it neat and clean. Put all materials away.
3. Begin with Activity Card #1. Good luck!

SAMPLE ACTIVITY CARD

Wildlife Management

Complete any two of the following:

1. Look through the information in the folder entitled "Wildlife Management." Also look up this topic in the books and magazines provided at the center. Then list and describe in a written report at least five ways that wildlife is currently being protected.
2. Do research on your own and write a brief report on your state's wildlife management programs. Respond to the following questions in your report:
   a. Where does the state agency get funds? What are some other possible sources of revenue?
   b. What are some of the agency's responsibilities?
   c. What wildlife-related positions does the agency have? What training would you need to work there?
   d. What are some of your state's main wildlife problems?
   e. What are some outstanding wildlife management successes in your state? What are some failures?
3. Interview a wildlife specialist (a ranger, biologist, researcher, zookeeper, etc.). Write an account of your interview, including qualifications for the position, job description, and the particular person's job-related problems and successes.
4. Visit a wildlife refuge and write a report describing what is being done there to help our wildlife.

DNA molecule: structure and replication

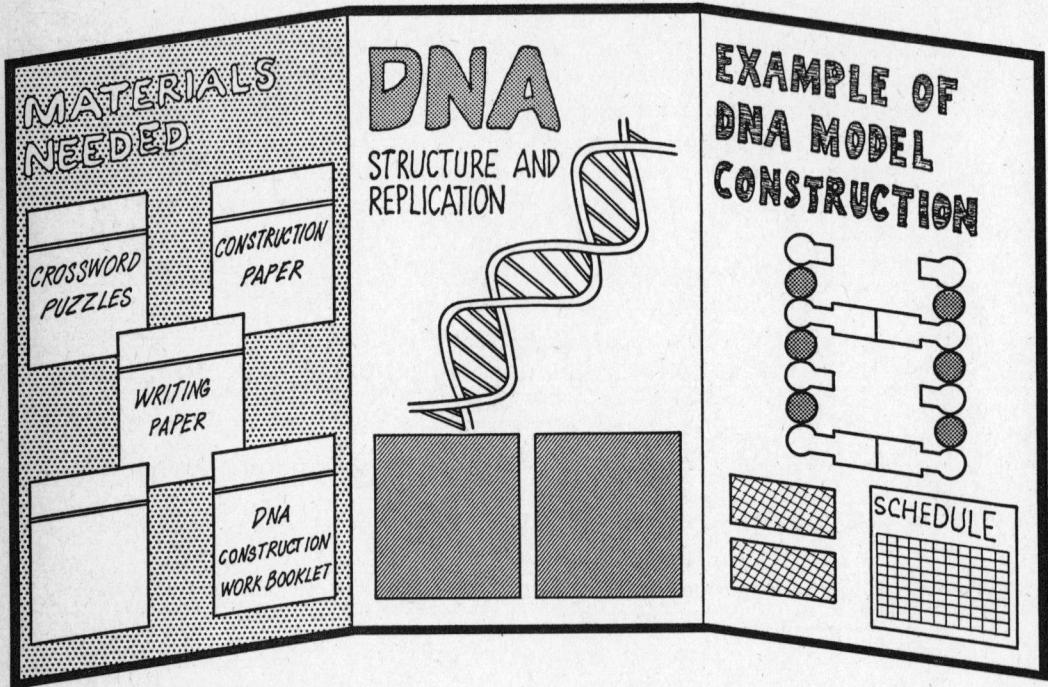

STUDENT OBJECTIVES

After working at this center, the student will be able to:

1. Describe the DNA molecule
2. Construct a DNA molecule given a unique base sequence
3. Name four nitrogen bases found in DNA
4. Name three subunits found in DNA
5. Define a nucleotide
6. Describe and give the significance of the chemical bonds found in the DNA molecule

7. Explain why we are all so different if we all have the same four nitrogen bases in our DNA
8. Pair nitrogen bases properly
9. Define genetic code

DIRECTIONS TO FOLLOW

The following tasks should be completed in the order given:

1. Go through the programmed learning packet on the structure of the DNA

DIRECTIONS (continued)

molecule. Be sure to keep the answers covered until you have made your response. If your answer is incorrect, reread the paragraph until you understand the given answer.

2. Complete the review section—check your answers with those provided. (Do not go on to the next activity until you feel confident you understand DNA.)

3. Complete the DNA construction project using the materials provided in the learning center.

4. If you desire extra credit, complete the crossword puzzle supplied.

5. Complete the summary questionnaire.

6. When you finish each activity, place a check on the activity schedule located at the center. When you have finished all the activities, turn in the following to your teacher:

a. The answer sheet for the programmed material

b. The DNA construction project

c. The summary questionnaire

d. The crossword puzzle (if you elected to do it for extra credit)

SAMPLE ACTIVITY CARD

DNA Construction Project

The object of this project is to make a DNA molecule that illustrates all of the features that you learned about in the programmed learning packet. Here is how the cell makes DNA:

1. The cell makes molecules of the three basic subunits found in a DNA molecule:
   a. Phosphate group
   b. Deoxyribose sugar molecule group.
   c. Four different types of nitrogen-containing bases.

2. One phosphate, one sugar, and one of the four bases combine to form a unit called a *nucleotide*.

3. Many nucleotides join to make a long DNA molecule.

To make a model DNA molecule, follow these directions carefully:

1. Select a DNA sequence card from the box—this will tell the sequence of the DNA strand you will construct. (Be sure to note the number on the card on your paper so your instructor can check your work.) Each card will have a sequence of five bases.

2. Cut out the proper shapes for the five bases as pictured below. Use the colors indicated. Keep the size of the bases uniform so that you may combine molecules later. On one of each type, write out the molecular structure of the molecule represented by that shape and color.

3. When you have completed all of the necessary subunits, attach them together to make a nucleotide. Bond the nucleotides together to make a short strand of DNA in your particular sequence. Make certain you bond only the correct bases together.

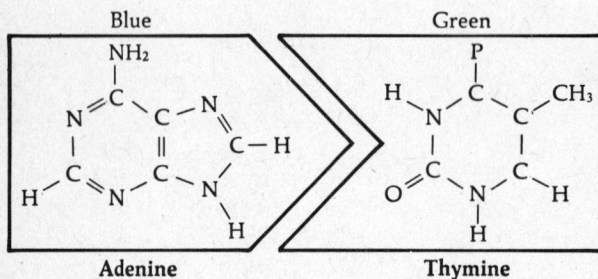

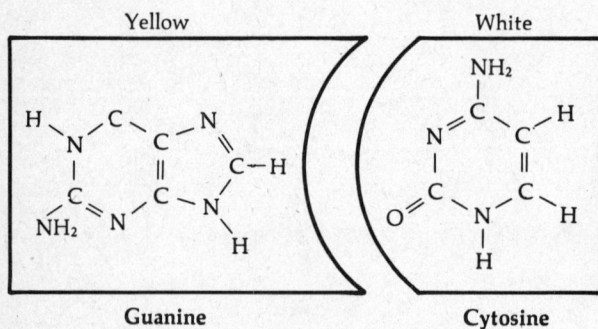

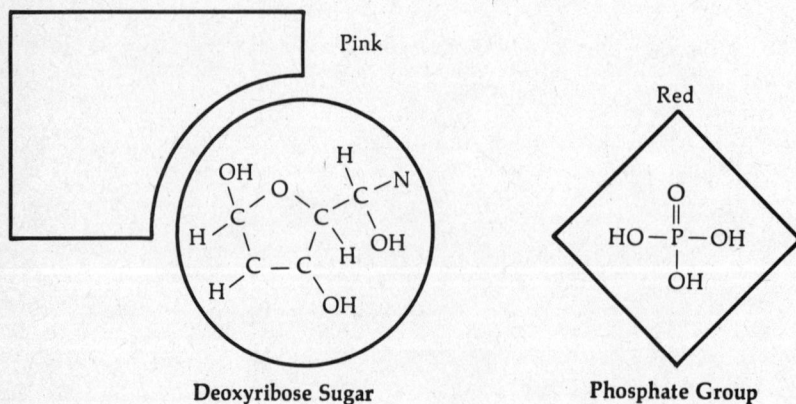

Blue

NH₂ — Adenine structure

Adenine

Green

Thymine structure with P, CH₃

Thymine

Yellow

Guanine structure with NH₂

Guanine

White

NH₂ — Cytosine structure

Cytosine

Pink

Deoxyribose sugar structure

Deoxyribose Sugar

Red

$$HO-P-OH$$ phosphate structure with O and OH

Phosphate Group

4. When completed, check your name off the schedule and turn your DNA model into the teacher to be checked. If your model is not correct, you will be asked to make another model.

constructing a project for the science fair

STUDENT OBJECTIVES

At this center, the student can:

1. Pick a science topic
2. Decide on a title
3. Determine necessary materials
4. Develop the project procedure
5. Collect appropriate data
6. Draw pertinent conclusions
7. Complete a written presentation of the project

SAMPLE ACTIVITY CARD

Let's Go to the Fair!

1. Study the *Student Guide* to find out which projects have been developed for the district science fair in the past.
2. Become familiar with the "Science Project Description" forms. Both blank and sample copies are available for your use.
3. Use the slide magnifier to view slides of last year's science fair projects.

---

the human digestive system

STUDENT OBJECTIVES

At this center the student will learn:

1. The anatomy and physiology of the human digestive system
2. The difference between intracellular and extracellular digestion
3. The organs and glands involved in human digestion
4. The chemicals and enzymes involved in digestion
5. The final products of digestion and how and where they are absorbed

SAMPLE ACTIVITY CARD

Parts of the Human Digestive System

1. Read Chapter three of your textbook, paying special attention to the diagrams.
2. Using a separate piece of paper, name and describe the function of each part of the human digestive system depicted below.
3. Be able to trace, step-by-step, the sequence of food as it passes through the stages of digestion.

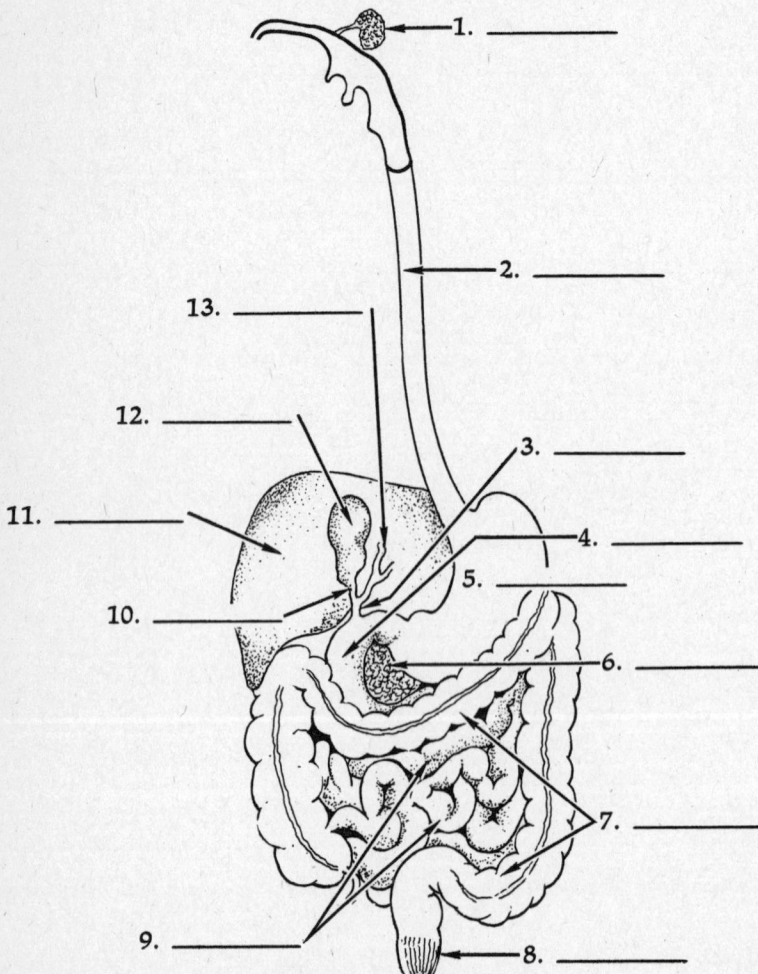

ANSWER KEY:

The activity card has been designed for students—this answer key has been placed here for the reader's convenience.

1. Salivary gland
2. Esophagus
3. Common bile duct
4. Duodenum
5. Stomach

6. Pancreas
7. Large intestine
8. Rectum
9. Small intestine

10. Cystic duct
11. Liver
12. Gallbladder
13. Hepatic duct

volcanoes

STUDENT OBJECTIVES

After going through the activity cards and resource material, you will be able to do the following:

1. Define *volcano*
2. Classify volcanoes according to activity (active, dormant, extinct)
3. Classify volcanic mountains and describe how each was formed (shield volcanoes, cinder cones, composite cones)
4. Describe various types of volcanic eruptions (Hawaiian, Strombolian, Vulcanian, Peleean, Plinian, Phreatic)
5. Identify and describe phenomena closely related to volcanoes that cause death and destruction (mudflows, tsunamis, earthquakes)
6. Define *lava* and *magma* and differentiate between the two
7. Describe the effects caused by the differing levels of silicon dioxide in the magma
8. Locate where the majority of the world's volcanoes are found and explain why this is so
9. Identify the various substances found in volcanic gas
10. Distinguish between the two types of lava flows
11. Describe the formation of lava tubes and lava trees
12. List the benefits that volcanoes provide humans
13. Relate some of the legends that various people associate with volcanoes

SAMPLE ACTIVITY CARD

Building a Volcano*

1. Work in groups of four or five for this project.
2. Take some of the modeling clay and mold it into the shape of a volcano cone.
3. Leave a small circular hole in the top so that "erupting lava" can force its way out.
4. Place your volcano on a metal baking sheet.
5. Build a shelf of clay about one inch below the top of the mouth of your volcano.
6. Obtain a test tube of ammonium dichromate from the teacher. Pour the contents into the mouth of the volcano.
7. When *all* groups are at this point, the room will be darkened.
8. One member of each group will light a match and hold it to the ammonium dichromate until it ignites. Observe the clouds of lavalike ash which should fall back around your volcano, building a cinder cone around the vent.

*This activity should be completed as a class project.

entomology

STUDENT OBJECTIVES

After completing this center, you will be able to:

1. Explain why insects are so important in the biosphere
2. Explain the beneficial and harmful effects of insect activities to man
3. Distinguish between the characteristics of crustaceans, myriapods, and arachnids, and tell how these animals are related to insects
4. Explain how crustaceans, myriapods, arachnids, and insects are believed to have evolved
5. List the problems insects had to overcome as terrestrial animals and explain how they solved these problems
6. Correctly label the most important anatomical features of insects
7. Identify the orders Coleoptera, Diptera, Hymenoptera, Lepidoptera, and Odonata
8. Recognize the distinguishing characteristics of these orders

SAMPLE ACTIVITY CARD

Insects

1. Take the worksheet entitled "Characteristics of Insects" from the pocket located on the center.
2. Using the information you have learned from the slides and tape, along with the bottled specimens, correctly complete the worksheet.
3. Place the completed worksheet in the box marked "Work Completed" located at the center.

Worksheet
Characteristics of Insects

1. Give at least two reasons why studying insects is important. Explain their importance in ecosystems and their beneficial and harmful effects to man.
2. What would the world be like without insects?
3. Fill in the following chart with the characteristics of each type of arthropod you have examined.

	Number of antennae	Number of legs	Number of body segments	Other characteristics
Crustaceans				
Myriapods				
Arachnids				
Insects				

4. What types of animals belong to the four insect groups of arthropods—Crustaceans, Myriapods, Arachnids, and Insects?

5. Define the following words:
   a. Morphology–
   b. Taxonomy–
   c. Lateral–
   d. Ventral–
   e. Dorsal–
   f. Exoskeleton–
6. Briefly trace the evolutionary development of the spider and the insect, listing all of the important animals and the time periods in which they lived.
7. What were the problems insects had to overcome as terrestrial animals? How did the insects manage to solve these problems?
8. Why was the development of wings so important for insects?
9. How do insects breathe?
10. Odonata—What does it mean to say that dragonflies are diurnal?
11. Diptera—What system have mosquitoes developed to suck your blood more efficiently? Why can their bite be dangerous?
12. Hymenoptera—What is an ovipositor? What has become of the ovipositor in some wasps?
13. Coleoptera—Why are ladybug beetles commercially valuable?

maps: the geographer's blueprints

STUDENT OBJECTIVES

When the student finishes with this center, he or she will be able to:

1. Read compass directions on maps and globes
2. Identify land masses known as continents
3. Locate large bodies of water in the world
4. Locate various countries within the seven continents
5. Identify major rivers in the world
6. Describe and demonstrate the use of longitude and latitude, including the six major imaginary lines
7. Read and interpret various legends, scales, and symbols on globes, maps, and charts

DIRECTIONS TO FOLLOW

1. Read all of the directions before beginning any of the activities.

DIRECTIONS (continued)

2. Take Activity Card #1 from the pocket on the learning center. Complete all tasks. Put the card back into the pocket.
3. Do the same with the rest of the activity cards. Follow the numerical sequence.
4. Make sure that all materials are replaced before leaving the center.

SAMPLE ACTIVITY CARD

Using the Globe

1. Find the legend on a flat map. Now find the legend on the globe. Compare the two legends. Be ready to relate any similarities and differences you find to the teacher.
2. Locate the time scale on the globe and discuss why it is necessary.
3. Study the land elevations in the legend. Why is there a need for topography in the legend?
4. Take a worksheet entitled "Using the Globe" from the box and complete each question. When this is completed, give it to the teacher.

Worksheet
Using the Globe

1. Locate the Amazon River Into what ocean does it flow? _____

   Why does it flow into that ocean? _____

   _____

2. Locate the Columbia River. Through what state does this river flow?

   _____ Where is the mouth of the

   Columbia? _____

3. Find the Amur River. Does it flow into the Pacific Ocean? _____

4. Into what sea does the Yangtse River flow? _____

   Where does it begin? _____

5. Locate these cities and name the country they are in.

1. Yokohama _____ 6. Shanghai _____

2. Vladivostok _____ 7. Hong Kong_____

3. Seoul _____ 8. Bangkok _____

4. Batavia _____ 9. Rome _____

5. Melbourne _____ 10. Vancouver _____

6. Which cities, of the above, are located opposite California on the globe?

_____

Which is the furthest away? _____ Which city is located

nearest Antarctica? _____ Which cities are close to the

Equator? _____

7. Through what sea would you need to sail to get from Hong Kong to

Manila? _____ From Vladivostok to Nagasaki? _____

From Sydney to Manila? _____

8. Find the International Date Line on the globe. Through which group of

islands does it pass in the South Pacific? _____

Which is nearer the date line, the Fiji Islands or Tahiti? _____

9. Locate the Solomon Islands. Through what sea would you need to sail

from there to Marlborough, Australia?_____

10. Are the Solomon Islands east or west of New Guinea? _____

11. In which direction would you need to sail to take a voyage from Guadal-
canal to New Caledonia? _____

12. The Suez Canal connects what two bodies of water?

_____ and _____

13. The Strait of Gibralter connects what two bodies of water?

_____ and _____

14. The Panama Canal connects what two bodies of water?

_____ and _____

patriot or revolutionary?

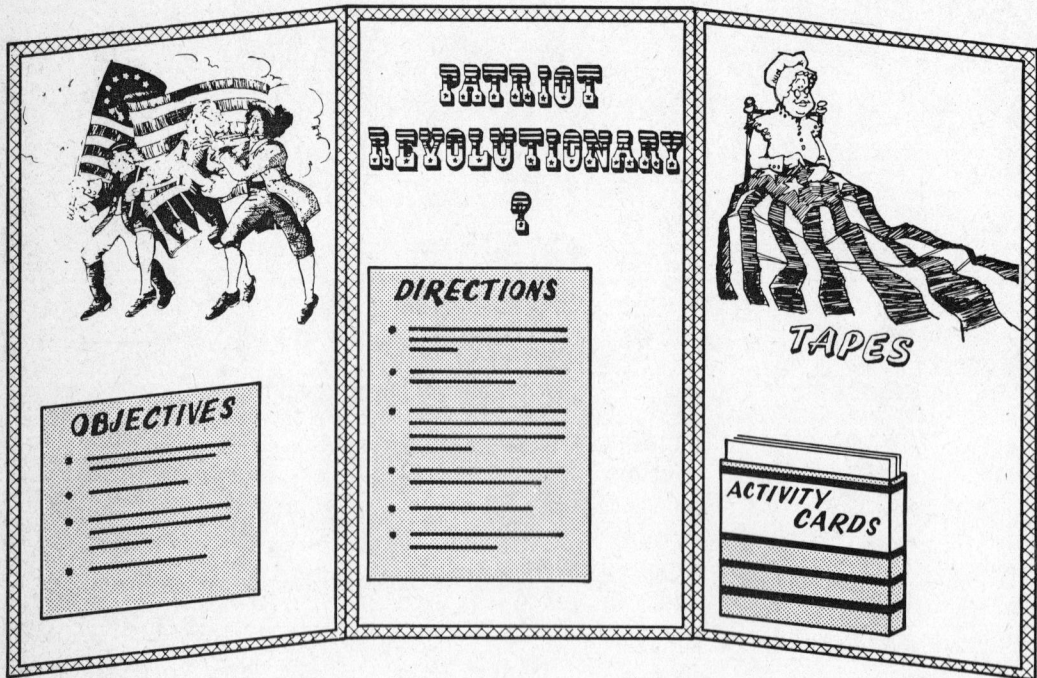

STUDENT OBJECTIVES

This center is about specific individuals who were involved in the events that led to the colonial fight for independence. Included among others were John Adams, Samuel Adams, Benedict Arnold, Patrick Henry, Thomas Jefferson, King George, Paul Revere, Thomas Paine, George Washington, and Peter Zenger.

After completing the activities in this center, the student will be able to:

1. Explain in detail the contribution made for or against the American Revolution by at least one of the individuals
2. List and describe a chronology of events that led up to the beginning of the Revolution
3. Describe the position taken by England toward the colonists
4. Present justification for declaring a person a *patriot* or a *revolutionary*

OBJECTIVES (continued)

5. Draw an analogy between the American Revolution and a 20th century "revolution" by identifying similarities of cause, events, and people.

DIRECTIONS TO FOLLOW

There are many materials and activities in this center: folders, a cassette, a filmstrip, books, posters, and worksheets. To help you locate appropriate aids, all materials have been color coded. For example, the activity card for Thomas Paine is color coded with a red flag in the upper right hand corner, and all source materials related to Thomas Paine also have this red flag code. Some materials will have more than one code since they are pertinent to more than one patriot.

Begin with Activity Card #1 which has a cassette explaining the purpose of the center and the options available to you. This center is self-contained and you should have no problem working through the activities on your own. If you do have a problem, however, please see the teacher.

SAMPLE ACTIVITY CARD

Benedict Arnold

1. Assume you are the prosecuting attorney in the judicial case against Benedict Arnold. Prepare a legal brief of questions that you would ask the defendant Arnold when he took the stand. (List your questions on a sheet of paper.)
2. Write a two-page summary of your case as the prosecuting attorney in the Benedict Arnold case. Remember, you are trying to convince the jury that Arnold is guilty. Be certain to state specific charges and concrete evidence to support your position.

---

an invitation to the Philippines

STUDENT OBJECTIVES

Participants in this center will be able to:

1. Locate the various cities and islands of the Philippines
2. Describe various customs, foods, and recreational activities
3. Present an oral and written report on one segment of Filipino history

SAMPLE ACTIVITY CARD

Customs, Foods, and Recreational Activities

1. You will find included at this center a carousel of slides and a cassette tape on the topics of customs, foods, and recreational activities. You will also need a pencil and paper.
2. Follow the direction card on the cover of the slide/tape box carefully.
3. Listen and respond to the directions you hear on the tape.
4. When you have finished with the slides and tape, take a copy of the worksheet "Customs, Foods, and Recreational Activities." Complete the worksheet. (If you need to review the slides or tape, please do so.)

Leonardo da Vinci: portrait of a Renaissance man

STUDENT OBJECTIVE

At this center the student will experience an in-depth exposure to the genius of Leonardo da Vinci.

SAMPLE ACTIVITY CARD

Leonardo Superstar

1. Read "Leonardo Superstar," a reprint from *Reader's Digest.*
2. On a separate piece of paper, write short answers to the following questions:
   a. What is an apprentice?
   b. During da Vinci's apprenticeship, what techniques did he master?
   c. Why would you say that Leonardo was gifted?
   d. Why do we know so much about him today?
3. Be prepared to discuss the following orally in class:
   a. Why can we say that during the period of the Renaissance, the modern world was born?
   b. What one single accomplishment impressed you the most about Leonardo?
   c. Why did da Vinci believe that art and science were the same?
   d. Do you believe that the same holds true in our world today? Why or why not? Explain.

Black Americans

STUDENT OBJECTIVES

After completing the activities in this center, the student will be able to:

1. Demonstrate the use of library reference skills
2. List and describe five Black people and their contributions to society
3. Write a short biography of one famous Black American
4. Write a letter to a publishing company that has not treated minority groups justly in its publications

SAMPLE ACTIVITY CARD

Writing a Biography

1. This activity is designed so that you can develop a "life book" on a famous Black American of your choice. The short written biography of the person you select should be accompanied with pictures. The length of your final project is up to you. However, be as complete as possible.
2. You can write about one of the five persons you investigated earlier or you might want to select a totally new person, one you have not yet researched.
3. During your library research, take notes on 3 x 5 cards. Some are located at the center.
4. Do not cut pictures from magazines or books located at the center or in the library. Find your own sources or draw your own pictures.
5. Your final copy should be written in ink and given to your teacher.

---

the world of work

STUDENT OBJECTIVES

At this center you will be able to:

1. Clarify information regarding personal interests and aspirations
2. List and describe the twelve major career cluster areas and explore the wide range of career options available
3. Experience the process of job entry by completing various job application materials
4. Write a job resumé for personal use
5. Develop an understanding of the world of work by describing:
   a. Why people work
   b. How people work
   c. What are tools
   d. How *work* became *employment*
   e. What causes unemployment

SAMPLE ACTIVITY CARD

Writing a Resumé

This activity card is designed to help you write a personalized resumé. This can be a valuable asset when you look for a job. Many resumés use the following components:

Name:	**Education:** (Grade level, schools attended, course of study followed)
Address:	
Telephone:	**Hobbies and Interests:**
Date of Birth:	**Previous work experience:** (Be specific— name of employer, address, telephone)
Height:	
Weight:	**References:** (Those who know you—work references, character references)

1. Look at the sample resumés located at the learning center. Discover similarities and differences between them. Which of the samples would you prefer your resumé to resemble?
2. Now, write a resumé using any of the above components that you believe appropriate.

handbuilding in clay

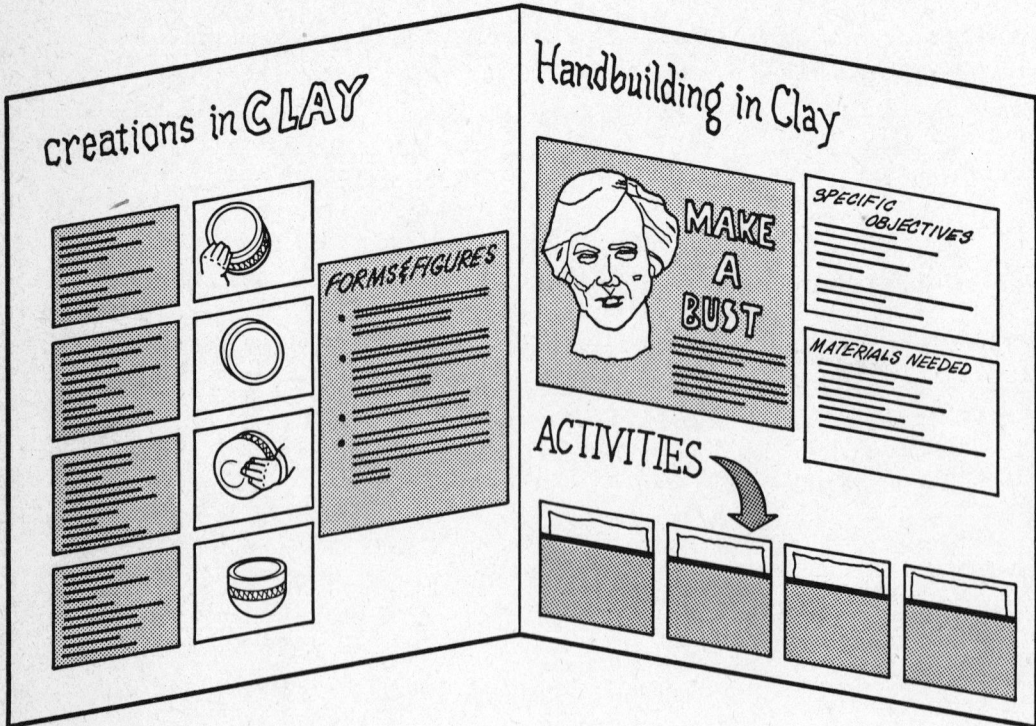

STUDENT OBJECTIVES

After using this center, the student will be able to:

1. Describe the properties and potentials of clay
2. Demonstrate the four methods of working with clay: adding on clay, scratching into clay, using texture stamps, and working with fingers
3. Create clay forms using the basic slab, coils, and pinch methods
4. List and describe the tools and equipment used when working with clay
5. Demonstrate the use of firing processes of both bisque and glaze kilns
6. Design and construct a major clay project (e.g., jar, pot, wind chime, vase, tile, etc.)

DIRECTIONS TO FOLLOW

1. Most of your work will be completed at your table and not at this center. Use the center for ideas, examples, and directions.
2. You must do all of the assignments on activity cards one through four.
3. After you have finished with Activity Card #4, you may select any one of the remaining six activity cards. This choice will be your major project. Be certain to take and read the worksheets that accompany the activity card that you choose.
4. Keep this center neat and clean.

SAMPLE ACTIVITY CARD

Working with Coils

What can I make out of coils? It can be functional or nonfunctional. A lidded jar, vase, goblet, free form, mug, cup, pitcher, bowl, container, planter, bottle, etc. and on, and on . . .

1. How to start:
   a. Make a slab of clay for desired shape of bottom of coiled form and build up from there

   OR

   b. Start with a coil that is tightly curled and build up from there.
2. How to build up:
   a. Take cigar-shaped wads of clay and roll with hands to create ropelike forms—about ½ inch thickness in diameter. Start from center and roll outwards.
   b. Place coil on top edge of the base. Weld the coil to the base by dragging small amounts of clay coils across the joints to seal it completely.
   c. Place each coil on top of next and continue process. (Make sure joints are at different places and not all lined up to prevent fracture lines and bad looks.)
3. How to change directions of sides of form (inward or outward):
   a. Inward—coils are placed toward the inner edges of the preceding coils.
   b. Outward—place each coil toward outer edge of the preceding coil.
4. How coils can be creative:

   Coils can just go around and around
   or they can go up and down.
   They can be fat or tall,
   and even made with little balls.
   Spirals can give a good effect.
   If you have other ideas please interject,
   And if you remember all those nice long lectures,
   YOU CAN EVEN ADD SOME FANCY TEXTURES.

---

5. How textures can be added:
    a. By stamping with texture tools
    b. By adding on pieces of clay
    c. By working with fingers
    d. By scratching into clay
6. Remember the elements and principles of design and use them to create unique, exciting, unbelievable coil forms!!! Use the sheet on wind chimes for definition of words. Ask your teacher for specific techniques.

macrame . . . why knot!

STUDENT OBJECTIVES

After using the macrame learning center, the student will:

1. Be able to describe some of the history of macrame
2. Be able to do the two basic macrame knots—the square knot and the half hitch
3. Have made a sample necklace
4. Have made one or more macrame projects

SAMPLE ACTIVITY CARD

The History of Macrame

1. Read the article "Macrame . . . Past and Present," that is located at the center.
2. When you have finished, take and complete one of the worksheets also entitled, "Macrame . . . Past and Present."

Worksheet
Macrame . . . Past and Present

1. Give two examples of the earliest knotted fabrics.

   _____ and _____

2. The word macrame probably comes from the Arabic word _____

   which means _____ or _____ .

3. Macrame means _____ in the Italian language.

4. Macrame was brought by the _____ to Spain during

   their _____ of that country.

5. Around 1850, macrame was used in Italy for _____

   _____ , _____

   and _____ .

6. Macrame was exported to _____ and ____ .

7. _____ and _____ in the Mediterranean

   area taught _____ to young boys and girls.

8. _____ of some kind is found in most cultures.

9. Much of the credit for the spread of macrame goes to _____

   of religious orders. _____ should also be given some
   of this credit.

10. _____ found macrame a worthwhile way of
    spending the idle hours on a long sea voyage.

11. List 3 things that sailors made with macrame:

    _____

12. These knotted articles were used for _____ when

    sailors went ashore on the _____ coast, in

    _____ , and in _____ .

13. Macrame has become very popular in the last _____ years.

14. Macrame is now used to decorate our _____ and _____ .

15. List 8 things that we now make with macrame.

color wheel

STUDENT OBJECTIVES

At this center you can:

1. Make a color wheel
2. Mix primary colors to produce secondary colors
3. Demonstrate what color combinations produce other colors
4. Recognize and differentiate among various colors
5. Use contrasting colors—light/dark, rough/smooth, bright/dull, and warm/cool—in your artwork

SAMPLE ACTIVITY CARD

Primary and Secondary Colors

1. Take a piece of paper, 8½ x 11, and fold it into three sections.
2. Paint one section red, one section yellow, and one section blue. These colors are called primary colors.
3. Now take another piece of paper and fold it into three sections.
4. Mix each combination of two of your primary colors together. What color appears when you mix:

   > Red and yellow?
   >
   > Red and blue?
   >
   > Yellow and blue?

5. Paint one section of your second piece of paper green, one section purple, and one section orange. These colors are called secondary colors.
6. When you have finished, put your work in your folder, clean your palette and brush, and put all materials away.

---

perspective drawing

STUDENT OBJECTIVES

After completing the activities in this center, students will be able to:

1. Draw one- and two-point perspective boxes
2. Draw one- and two-point perspective buildings with windows, doors, and lettering
3. List terms related to perspective drawing
4. Apply methods other than perspective to make objects look three dimensional

SAMPLE ACTIVITY CARD

Drawing Boxes

1. Look at the examples provided in the folder marked "Perspective Boxes."
2. Draw nine two-point perspective boxes—three at eye level, three above eye level, and three below eye level.
3. When you have completed these drawings, give them to the teacher.

type right

STUDENT OBJECTIVES

At this center the student will be able to:

1. Review proper typewriting techniques, correct fingering, and the parts of a typewriter
2. Review tabulation principles and how to put these principles to use
3. Evaluate present speed and accuracy status and set goals for future progress
4. Evaluate present knowledge of typewriting rules and forms

DIRECTIONS TO FOLLOW

1. Only two students should work at this center at one time.
2. Before you begin the activities, look at the center and the parts it contains.
3. There are ten activity cards at this center. Do all of these activities in numerical order.
4. Keep all of your work in your file folder.
5. Ask your teacher for help if it is needed.
6. Keep the center neat and clean.

SAMPLE ACTIVITY CARD

Know Your Typewriter

The following activities are designed so that you can review the principal parts of the typewriter along with its various functions and uses. There are three worksheets located at the center that are part of this activity card:

Typing Pre-test
Typewriter Check Sheet
Tabulation Principles

1. Do the worksheets in numerical order.
2. When you have completed each worksheet, use the answer key found in the "Answer Folder" at the center. Correct all errors.

Worksheet
Typewriter Check Sheet

1. Using the typewriter instruction booklet located at the center, fill in the following information as you locate and learn to operate the various parts:

   Name of typewriter _____

   Model _____

   Type size _____

   Strokes per inch _____

   Carriage size _____

2. Locate the following:
   a. Space bar
   b. Margin set
   c. Ribbon controls
   d. Ribbon reverse
   e. Tab set key(s)
   f. Tab clear key
   g. Platen control for multiple copies
   h. Margin release
   i. Automatic keys
   j. Backspace key

3. Answer the following questions:
   a. What is the paper-guide setting for 8½ x 11 paper?
   b. What is the center of the page?
   c. Using a page that is 6 x 10, what is the correct paper-guide setting?
   d. Where is the center of a 6 x 10 page?
4. List the special features of this typewriter.

letter corner

STUDENT OBJECTIVES

At this center the student will learn to write business letters using the following formats.

1. Inverted style
2. Semi-block style
3. Modified block style
4. Full block style
5. Indented style

SAMPLE ACTIVITY CARD

Six Parts of a Business Letter

The six parts of a business letter are as follows:

Heading—Your address: number, street, city, state, zip code
The date: month, day, year

Inside Address—Name and full address of business firm or person to whom you are writing

Salutation—Formal style greeting (Gentlemen:, Dear Sir:)

Body—The message or content of the letter

Closing—The formal closing phrase (Sincerely, Very truly yours)

Signature—Your name written in ink below the closing phrase

1. Heading

2. Inside Address

3. Saluation

4. Body

5. Closing

6. Signature

**Business
Letter
Sample
Form**

Your Name
Number, Street
City, State, Zip Code

Education Products Corporation
605 First Street
Grand Haven, Michigan 92119

**Envelope
Sample
Form**

Your activity is to write a letter to any real business. Part of your task is to seek a response to your letter. You might want to write a letter requesting a free sample of a product or to seek general information. Follow the format provided on this activity card. Remember to include all six parts in your business letter and to prepare a proper envelope.

When you have completed your letter, check your work with your teacher before mailing. When you receive the reply to your letter, share this with your teacher, too.

hand sewing

QUILTING

Hand Sewing

PATTERNS

DIRECTIONS

ACTIVITY CARDS

STUDENT OBJECTIVES

After working at this center, the student will be able to:

1. Recognize the basic hemstitches
2. Select and use a proper thimble when sewing
3. Sew the basic hemstitches
4. Demonstrate proper sewing methods for attaching fasteners (buttons, hooks and eyes, and snaps) and locate where each is used on a garment
5. Select and use the proper needle and thread for sewing on different types of fabrics
6. Demonstrate proper use of equipment
7. Demonstrate basic methods of hand-finishing seams
8. Recognize and judge well-made hems and hand-finished seams

DIRECTIONS TO FOLLOW

1. What can you do at the center?
   a. Select equipment needed to hand sew buttons, metal fasteners, hems, and finish seams
   b. Choose different fabrics for each of the sewing projects
   c. Work a puzzle on hand sewing to learn terms
   d. Sew various items onto fabric swatches
2. Each activity card is different. There is no order to follow. All cards should be completed.
3. All of the materials needed for the projects are labeled and found at the center.
4. Completed projects should be stapled to a sheet of notebook paper that contains your name and class period. Deposit completed projects in the envelope marked "Work Completed." All work that is not completed should be placed in the envelope marked "Work in Progress."
5. Begin with any of the activity cards. Remember to follow all instructions found on the activity cards.

SAMPLE ACTIVITY CARD

Hand Sewing Terms

1. Take a copy of the worksheet entitled "Find the Word."
2. Find and circle each of the words listed.

Worksheet
Find the Word

PINS	GAUGE	PINKED SCISSORS
BEESWAX	HEM	PINCUSHION
BUTTON	SHEARS	SEAM RIPPER
SNAP	NYLON	CATCH STITCH
COTTON	THIMBLE	CUTTING BOARD
NEEDLE	SILK	HOOK AND EYE
THREAD	RAYON	BUTTONHOLE TWIST
POLYESTER	WOOL	

Worksheet
Find the Word (continued)

```
O N H N T H E C S N I P J U O R S E H U M E
Z A S N A F G Y A S I R D T B E C C O M E S
P I N C U S H I O N R L T A O N T E N G T U
W I O N M F O U R S Q M A Z E U H J R A B I
T G I E Z C O T T O N O X N Z R Y K U U N M
E T H E S A L E E M P V O W U S H R T G Q E
A N M D V Y M O H R T N U P B O H T X E B D
R I A L O L I R M E R O A S U C O V W L R R
A E M E R X S R O S S I C S T N T U S O M A
S K E M I Q A H C I T P A I T E J R I N U O
E U H A J Y I J L M I V T L O L A A P Y A B
R A K E O V K C B E V S B K N E S L D G Q G
O B I N Z E J I Y A H E A N H K R F O B B N
R C Y U E P L E Y C Q A O S O Z R V B O E I
T O D G R M D J T S D M P M L I P E J H W T
H N Y L O N U A U B E R C Y E K E T S A J T
I U G W A D C R J R Q I N F T S B G I R L U
N E S K W E E N E O F P G T W C I C W D T C
T S O R E T S E Y L O P D A I T H I M B L E
S O C I T S N F U V K E X M S W O T I F P J
H I F O U H A D E Z K R O W T B E N A G U A
E N A M R W I S A N O T E X U A G I B U W C
G I O T S I T M I O C E N L A E W R M D N A
A C B E O Q I P S R K D S I M L R D S P A N
```

you are what you eat!

STUDENT OBJECTIVES

At this learning center the student will learn:

1. What nutrients are
2. Why we need nutrients
3. An easy method for securing needed nutrients
4. To classify foods into the Four-Food-Group System

5. To plan balanced meals using the Four-Food-Group System as a guide
6. How to analyze personal food selections to see if they meet the minimum requirements found in the system

SAMPLE ACTIVITY CARD

Classifying Mixed Foods

1. Take a copy of the chart "Classifying Mixed Foods" from the center.
2. Each food item listed on the chart contains more than one kind of food. Classify the foods by making a check under the food groups for each kind of food. If there are two separate foods from the same group in a single food item, make two checks (one for each food) in the appropriate column.
3. When you are finished, check your work with the answer key, and read the handout, "Classifying Mixed Foods." Then, go on to another activity card.

Chart
Classifying Mixed Foods

FOOD	MILK	MEAT	VEGE-TABLE/FRUIT	BREAD/CEREAL	EXTRA
A. Spaghetti and Meat Balls (spaghetti, meat, tomato sauce)		X	X	X	
B. Ham and Cheese Omelette (ham, cheese, eggs)	X	XX			
1. Macaroni and Cheese (macaroni, cheese)					
2. Beef Stew (meat, potatoes, gravy, carrots, onions)					
3. Peanut Butter and Jelly Sandwich (bread, jelly, peanut butter)					
4. Banana Split (banana, ice cream, topping, nuts, whipped cream)					
5. Taco (tortilla, beef, lettuce, tomato, cheese)					
6. Pizza (crust, tomato sauce, cheese, pepperoni)					
7. Cheeseburger (ground beef, bun, cheese, mustard, catsup)					
8. Egg Salad Sandwich (bread, egg, mayonnaise)					
9. Strawberry Shortcake (strawberries, biscuit, whipped cream)					
10. Chili Dog (hot dog, bun, ground meat, chili beans)					

la casa, por dentro

Display board showing: ESPAÑA (with text), mountains illustration, SPANISH COAT OF ARMS with emblem, españa map of Spain, SPANISH · NUMERO UNO, ACTIVITIES card, and a pocket holder.

STUDENT OBJECTIVES

After completing the activities in this center, the student will be able to use Spanish to:

1. Identify orally and in writing the various parts and rooms of a house
2. Identify orally and in writing various pieces of furniture found in a house
3. Participate, with a fluent speaker, in a dialogue about a specific situation concerning the house
4. Repeat a brief incident that concerns the house after hearing it told on the cassette tape

DIRECTIONS TO FOLLOW

1. Observe carefully how the center is arranged.
2. Complete all of the activity cards. Begin with Card #1. Follow the instructions provided.
3. Return all materials to their original location.
4. Keep the center neat and orderly.

SAMPLE ACTIVITY CARD

La Casa, Por Dentro

1. On 8½ x 11 paper, make a plan of your house. Be sure to include all of the major pieces of furniture and appliances.
2. Now carefully label, in Spanish, each piece of furniture and appliance in your house. Then make a list of these words on a separate sheet of paper.
3. Obtain a copy of the worksheet entitled "La Casa, Por Dentro" located at the center. Compare your list with the vocabulary provided. Are there pieces of furniture or appliances on the vocabulary list that you forgot to include in your house? If so, make you corrections now.

---

verbos Españoles

STUDENT OBJECTIVES

This center is designed for the review of verbs, both regular and irregular. By using a variety of listening, speaking, reading, and writing activities the student will be able to review and practice the verbs shown here.

Irregular Verbs

estar	venir	hacer
ir	ver	oir
salir	dar	poder
ser	decir	poner
tener	querer	saber

Regular Verbs

-er, -ir, and -ar

SAMPLE ACTIVITY CARD

To Be or Not To Be

1. Listen to Cassette Tape #1. Follow all instructions provided on the tape.
2. Obtain the worksheet "Ser e Estar" from the worksheet folder located at the center, and complete it.
3. Write five creative sentences using various forms of *Ser* and *Estar*.
4. Put all completed work in your folder. Include your worksheet and the creative sentences.
5. Rewind the cassette tape and put it back in the "tape pocket" at the center. Turn the recorder to "Off." Leave the center neat and clean.

---

first aid center

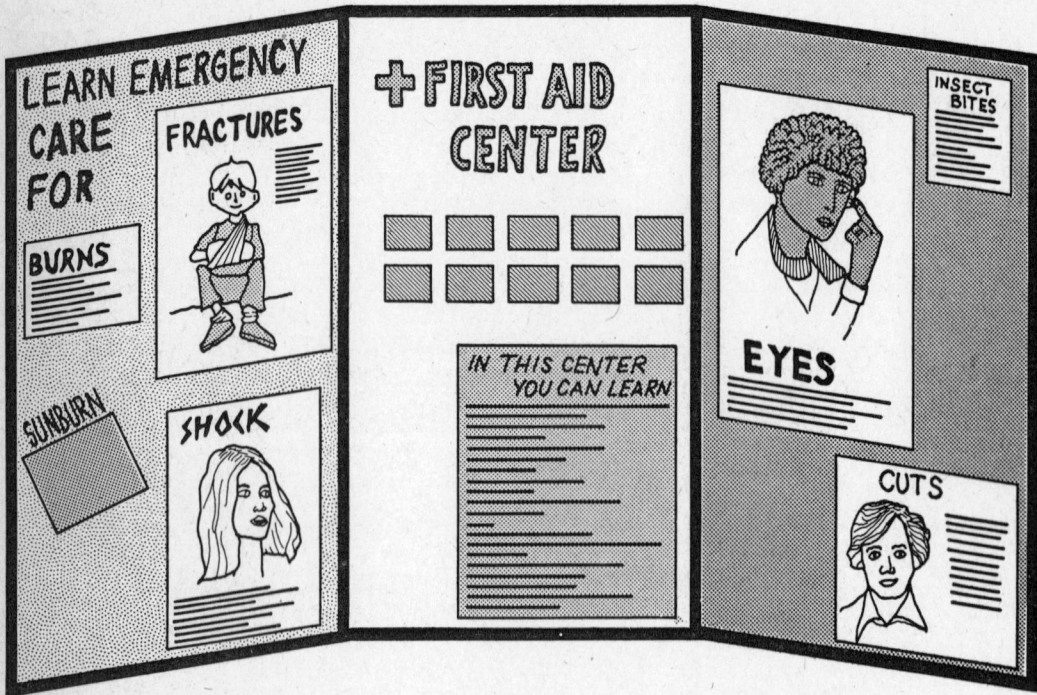

STUDENT OBJECTIVES

At this center the student will be able to:

1. Test his or her knowledge of first aid skills and become familiar with new skills
2. Practice first aid techniques
3. Create a simulated situation requiring first aid and develop a workable solution with the materials available

DIRECTIONS TO FOLLOW

1. This center uses both sides of the fold-away model learning center entitled "First Aid Center" and the other entitled "The Case of Careless Ken." Notice the parts of each, and the materials provided.
2. There are a total of five activity cards for this center. You must complete all five activities, although they do not have to be completed in order.

SAMPLE ACTIVITY CARD

First Aid Matching Game

1. Take a copy of the worksheet called "First Aid Matching Game" and complete it according to the instructions given.
2. Check your work with the answer sheet provided in the center. Make any necessary corrections.

Worksheet
First Aid Matching Game

Match Column I, situations requiring first aid, to Column II, first aid techniques or steps to be taken. Place the letter of the item from Column I next to the correct first aid technique in Column II in the space provided.

Column I

a. Bee Sting   e. Sprain   i. Shock
b. Nosebleed   f. Burn   j. Frostbite
c. Sunburn   g. Fracture
d. Poison plants   h. Cuts, scratches, abrasions

Column II

_____ 1. Submerge immediately in cold water or apply ice wrapped in a cloth. Continue treatment until pain is gone. Consult a physician.

_____ 2. Cover area with a warm hand, clothing, or blanket. Give victim a warm bath, encourage exercise.

_____ 3. Clean around area with soap and water, then wash area itself with soap. If necessary, remove foreign objects, then cover with clean cloth or sterile gauze.

_____ 4. Person should sit quietly with head thrown back for ten minutes. If problem continues, pack area with sterile gauze, have person lie down with head elevated, use cold wet towel on area.

_____ 5. Wash area with soap and water or rubbing alcohol. Cover with a dressing soaked in solution of baking soda or epsom salts.

　　　　　　　　 6. Remove cause of problem with sterilized needle or knife. Run cold water over and around area to relieve pain or pack with ice. Sponge with alcohol and apply calamine lotion.

　　　　　　　　 7. Apply cold cream or such oils or greases as salad oil or shortening.

　　　　　　　　 8. Immobilize with splints. Move as little as possible. Treat for shock.

　　　　　　　　 9. Keep patient lying down with head lower than feet. Loosen patient's clothing. Get patient to hospital as soon as possible.

　　　　　　　　 10. Elevate injured area to a comfortable position. Apply ice or a cold compress to area to reduce pain and swelling.

focus on breakfast

STUDENT OBJECTIVES

After using this learning center, the student will be able to:

1. Identify and describe what makes a good breakfast using the four basic food groups
2. Select substitutions of foods not normally eaten for breakfast
3. Develop a variety of balanced menus
4. Describe the proteins, minerals, and vitamins the body needs everyday for health protection and for growth

SAMPLE ACTIVITY CARD

Do You Eat Right?

Using the 5 x 8 cards found at the center, do the following:

1. Record everything you ate in the last four days.
2. Chart or graph the foods you ate into:
   a. Milk group
   b. Meat group
   c. Vegetable/fruit group
   d. Bread/cereal group
   e. Extra foods (those which do not fit into the first four groups)
3. Circle with a red pen those foods you liked best.
4. Circle with a green pen those foods you liked least.
5. Which day did you have the most balanced diet? Why? (Explain.)

cycle tune-up and service center

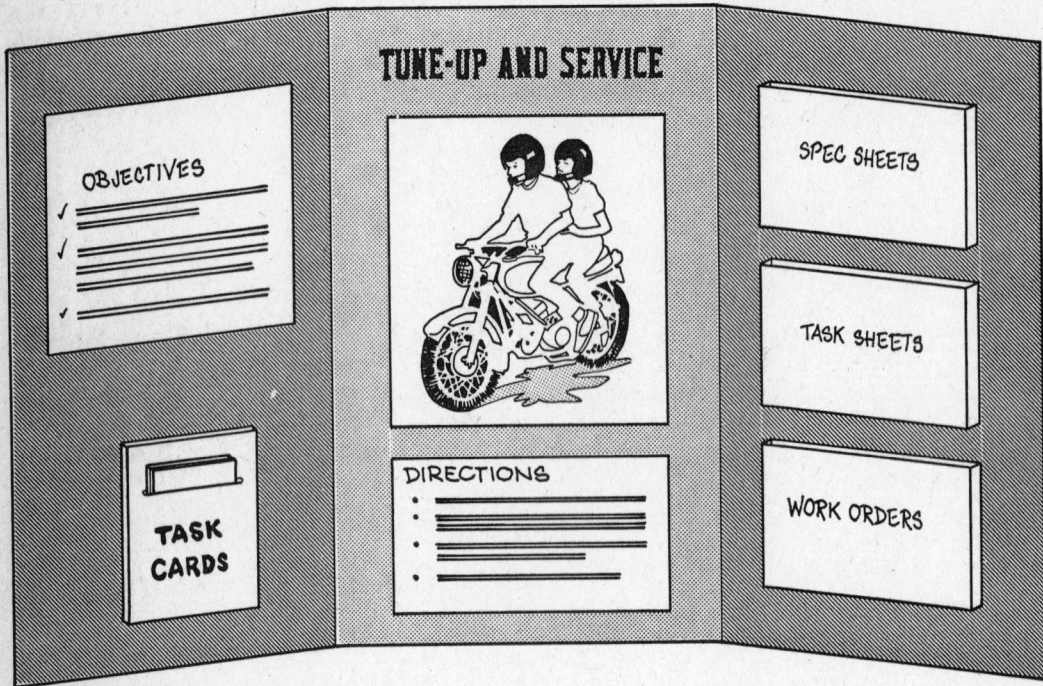

STUDENT OBJECTIVES

On completion of the activities of this learning center, you will be able to:

1. List all the tasks done as part of a full-service tune-up
2. Complete a full-service specification sheet
3. Perform the tasks comprising a full-service tune-up on a MT-250 Honda
4. Complete a work order including the parts list, additional work needed, recommendations to the customer, time spent, and mechanic's initial
5. Observe all safety rules associated with these tasks

DIRECTIONS TO FOLLOW

1. Before you begin the activities, look over the center and familiarize yourself with the location of the materials.

DIRECTIONS (continued)

2. No more than two students may work on this project at one time.
3. Complete all the tasks listed on the twenty activity cards.
4. Submit finished motorcycle, check-off sheet, and work order to instructor for evaluation.
5. Keep work area clean and return all materials to their proper location upon completion. This is your responsibility!

SAMPLE ACTIVITY CARD

Drain Transmission Oil

1. Check out a drain pan from the tool crib.
2. Remove the 17mm drain plug from the motorcycle and allow oil to drain into pan.
3. Continue draining oil while you go on to other activities. Leave this card on the work bench to remind you to refill transmission with oil.
4. Replace drain plug and fill transmission with the quart of oil provided.
5. Empty drain pan, wash out, and check back into crib.

---

resistor color codes

STUDENT OBJECTIVES

After working at this center, the student will be able to:

1. Determine the resistance of selected resistors by their color code

2. Use the Volt-Ohm Meter (VOM) to determine the resistance of selected resistors

SAMPLE ACTIVITY CARD

Using the Volt-Ohm Meter

1. On a separate piece of paper, list the colors and values of each resistor found at the center.
2. Check each resistor with the VOM and determine the tolerance. Add this information to your list.

Name _____   Score _____

	Colors	Value	VOM Value	Tolerance
1.				
2.				
3.				
4.				
5.				
6.				
7.				
8.				
9.				
10.				
11.				
12.				
13.				
14.				

3. Turn your list in to the teacher for scoring.

exploring the magic of music

STUDENT OBJECTIVES

The purpose of this four-sided learning center is to help you learn the fundamentals of music and to provide extra-credit projects with a variety of activities. At this center, you can:

1. Learn to read music (notes, beats, etc.)
2. Study music from other cultures
3. Identify and describe particular musical instruments within an orchestra section
4. Investigate famous composers
5. Make a musical instrument
6. Locate and describe famous music centers (schools, opera houses, etc.)
7. Play games such as music bingo, crossword puzzles, dominos with note values, word search, and computer notation

DIRECTIONS TO FOLLOW

1. Look at the center and note the parts it contains. Each of the four sections relate to a different music topic.

DIRECTIONS (continued)

2. Study the models and examples posted on the center.
3. Each activity card is different. There is no order to follow.
4. Complete at least two activity cards from each section.

SAMPLE ACTIVITY CARD

The Orchestra

1. Select a standard orchestral instrument and look it up in the resource material found at the center. Write a one- or two-page report based on your research, including a drawing of the instrument.
2. Select one orchestra section (winds, brass, strings, or percussion) and identify and illustrate each instrument in the section.
3. Draw a diagram of an orchestra, showing where each instrument is located in relation to the conductor.

African music

STUDENT OBJECTIVES

After working at this learning center, the student will be able to:

1. Identify various musical elements characteristic of African music
2. Recognize music as a functional part of African life
3. Identify names and sounds of African instruments
4. Respond artistically to sensations evoked by listening to African music
5. Recognize and describe the contribution and influence Africans have made to American music

SAMPLE ACTIVITY CARD

Designing an Album Cover

1. Listen to one of the tapes found at the center for a few minutes to get a feeling for the music.
2. Select several colors of paint from the center that seem appropriate to the music.
3. Assemble other necessary art supplies.
4. Begin listening to the tape again. While you listen, draw a design for an album cover for this music. Be creative and have fun!

---

bicycling

STUDENT OBJECTIVES

The general goals of this center are:

1. To provide the student with a general knowledge and understanding of bicycling and bicycle safety
2. To provide the student with a variety of self-directed and individualized learning opportunities relating to bicycling and bicycle safety
3. To develop student interest in bicycling that will have lifetime carry-over value

After completing the activities in this center, the student will be able to:

1. Explain what a gear ratio is
2. List ten safety rules for city riding
3. Identify eight major bike parts
4. Demonstrate the proper way to lock a bicycle
5. Demonstrate how to shift gears properly
6. Describe the location of one local bikeway or bike route

OBJECTIVES (continued)

7. Explain the way to inflate tires properly
8. Describe what *ankling* means
9. Explain how to determine frame size on a bicycle
10. Describe the four hand positions used with dropped handlebars

DIRECTIONS TO FOLLOW

1. Observe the center. Note the resource material.
2. Complete the activities outlined on the activity cards.
3. Keep the center neat and orderly.
4. Record your progress with the teacher.
5. Begin now with Activity Card #1.

SAMPLE ACTIVITY CARD

Parts of a Bicycle

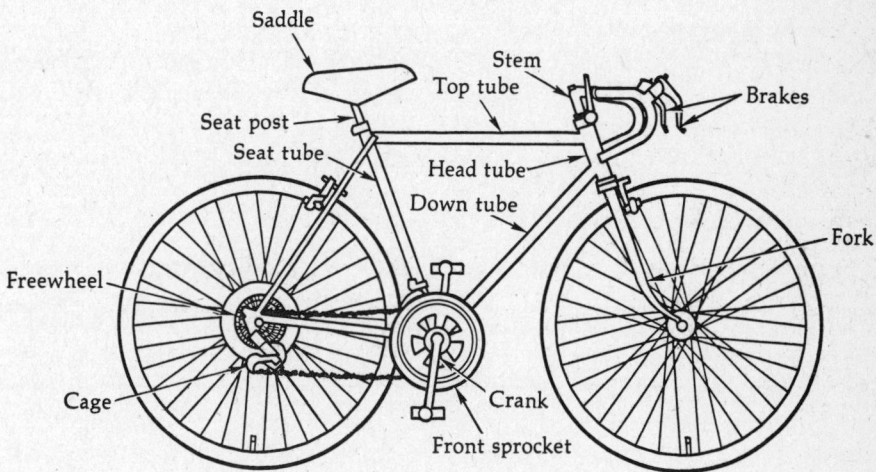

Saddle
Stem
Top tube
Brakes
Seat post
Seat tube
Head tube
Down tube
Fork
Freewheel
Cage
Crank
Front sprocket

1. Using any of the bicycling resource books found at the center, read and study the material on the function and parts of a 10-speed bicycle.
2. On a sheet of paper, list each bicycle part illustrated above, and describe the function it performs.
3. You also should be able to locate the above parts by name on any similar bicycle.

tennis everyone!

STUDENT OBJECTIVES

At this tennis center, the student will learn:

1. How to keep score
2. Basic rules for playing
3. Terminology used on the court
4. The differences and similarities of doubles and singles tennis
5. Basic skill strokes (forehand, backhand, and serve)

SAMPLE ACTIVITY CARD

Tennis Basics

1. Look at the illustrations posted on the center. Each is numbered and there are a total of fifteen. Each illustration presents either a rule of tennis and/or a basic skill stroke.
2. On a sheet of paper, number one through fifteen. Look at the illustration with the corresponding number and write down the rule and/or stroke shown. (Some will have both.)

   Example: 1. Rule: The ball landed in the doubles alley during a singles match. The shot was not good.
   Stroke: Forehand.

---

bump and boogie with volleyball!

STUDENT OBJECTIVES

At this center you can learn or review:

1. Basic volleyball skills
2. Rules of the game
3. Offensive systems
4. Defensive formats
5. How to set
6. The service

SAMPLE ACTIVITY CARD

Achieving a Mental Set

A set of slides has been developed that shows each phase of specific volleyball skills. The slides were prepared so that you can achieve a "mental set" by visualizing what is supposed to happen prior to performing the skill. A cassette tape has also been prepared so that you can hear about the skill. Ask your teacher for the slides and tape. You will need thirty minutes to secure the equipment, view the program, and return all materials.

After you have seen and heard about the various skills, you will need to practice them. There are other activity cards describing each skill and providing skill exercises. Begin practicing now with Activity Card #6.

Mr. Time

STUDENT OBJECTIVES

At this center you can learn:

1. The different parts and symbols of a clock
2. How many minutes are in one hour and in different parts of an hour
3. The position of the hour hand and minute hand at different times
4. How to express time in numbers and words

DIRECTIONS TO FOLLOW

1. You should have the cassette on "Play" as you read these directions. Be certain to properly plug in the earphones. The tape should be kept on throughout these activities to help guide you, except when it says to turn it off.*
2. Each activity card has problems for you to solve. Write your answers to the *solve* problems on the worksheets with

*This center is designed for use in a special education class. The student's reading of directions and activity cards is assisted by listening to the tape.

DIRECTIONS (continued)

the marking pen provided. Show your answers to the *show* problems on our clock, Mr. Time.

3. Check your answers for all the problems with the answer key.
4. If you answer any problem incorrectly, go back and look at the problem again to see where you made your mistake. If you still do not understand, check with your teacher.
5. When you have finished, turn the cassette player to "Off."

SAMPLE ACTIVITY CARD

What Time Is It?

1. This is the beginning of Activity Card #3.
2. Please get Activity Worksheet #3 located at the center.
3. Look at the examples at the top of the worksheet. The first example shows the time to be either 1:00 A.M. or 1:00 P.M. Notice that the long hand or hour hand points to the 12, and the short hand or minute hand points to the 1.
4. The second example shows either 6:00 A.M. or 6:00 P.M. Notice how we can express time in both numbers and words. Look carefully at the example.
5. Look at the other problems. You must *solve* them. Write your answers in the blanks provided on the worksheet just as in the examples shown above. Stop the tape while you solve the problems. Turn it on again when you have completed all of the *solve* problems. Check your answers with the answer key provided in "Mr. Time's" folder. Stop the tape now.
6. Now look at the *show* problems. *Show* your answers on Mr. Time.
7. This is the end of Activity Card #3. Please put all materials away neatly. Thank you. Turn off the tape recorder.

---

follow directions: from here --- to there

STUDENT OBJECTIVES

Upon completion of the activities found in this center, the student will be able to:

1. Locate information accurately and as needed in common publications such as telephone books, newspapers, reference books, transportation schedules, and catalogs

2. Follow directions for given maps, do-it-yourself projects, recipes, and puzzles

SAMPLE ACTIVITY CARD

Dividing A Square

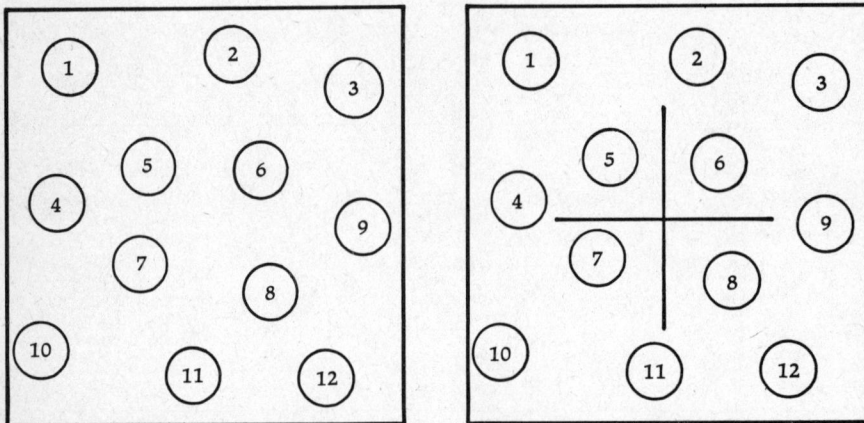

Draw a square on your paper marked with twelve circles as in the diagram to the left. The object of this puzzle is to cut the square into four pieces of similar shape and size, each piece to contain only three circles. Start by drawing crossed lines between circles 5, 6, 7, and 8, as in the diagram at the right above.

The remaining steps in solving the puzzle are as follows:

1. Draw a line under circles 1 and 2 from the edge of the square to meet the end of the line extending upward between circles 5 and 6.
2. Draw a line above circles 11 and 12 from the edge of the square to meet the end of the line extending downward between circles 7 and 8.
3. Draw a line from the edge of the square passing down between circles 2 and 3 to meet the end of the line running across the square between circles 6 and 8.
4. Draw a line from the edge of the square passing up between circles 10 and 11 to meet the end of the line running across the square between circles 5 and 7.
5. Count the number of pieces you have. How many circles appear in each piece? Are the pieces similar in size and shape? You may now cut the square into pieces.

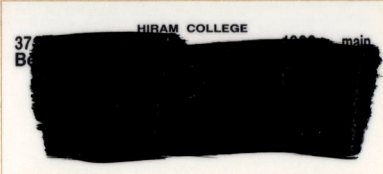